Liturgy and Education

Liturgy and Education

Massey H. Shepherd, Jr.

THE SEABURY PRESS

NEW YORK

ACKNOWLEDGMENTS

Grateful acknowledgment is made to the following authors and publishers for permission to use copyrighted material from the titles listed below:

Harper & Row, Publishers, New York—John Knox, *The Church and the Reality of Christ*

The Newman Press, Westminster, Maryland—St. Augustine, *The Teacher*

Oxford University Press, New York—Massey H. Shepherd, Jr., editor, *Worship in Scripture and Tradition,* for the quotations from the essays of Dean Alexander Schmemann and Professor Franklin W. Young

Preface

THE THEME of Liturgy and Education was suggested to the author in the invitation of the Trustees of the Lester Bradner Fund, since the lectureship which they administer is concerned with the general subject of Christian education. I am deeply grateful for the honor of this lectureship—the more so, as I have never thought of myself in any way as a specialist in the science of education, despite the fact that I have spent most of my adult life in the task of teaching in theological schools. What I have had to say, therefore, is basically an interpretation, from my studies and experiences, of the meaning of the liturgy; and this, I hope, reveals some indications of relevance to the process of our formation and discipline in Christian discipleship, which is the primary concern and problem of Christian education.

The substance of the book was originally delivered in four lectures at The General Theological Seminary in New York City, in February, 1964. I have thought it more helpful to the reader if in this published form I divided the materials into shorter chapter-units, and added here and there some modicum of documentation.

It is a pleasure to record and give expression to my heartfelt appreciation for all the gracious hospitality extended to me at the seminary by Dean Lawrence Rose and the faculty and students. They provided a happy home for me in the seminary

5

close for an extended period over and beyond the time required for the lectures themselves.

I should add, perhaps, that the last lecture, "Reconstruction of the Liturgy," happened to coincide with the meeting at the seminary of the Standing Liturgical Commission of the Protestant Episcopal Church. But it should in no way be interpreted as a pronouncement for or by the Commission itself.

M.H.S., JR.

Contents

PART

I

*Definition
of the
Liturgy*

I

Some Presuppositions:
Personal
and Theological

1] ONE'S conceptions and convictions regarding so large
a theme as the relation of Christian liturgy to education cannot be formulated and expounded out of a vacuum. This is
especially true in my case, since I have been engaged exis-
tentially in both of these endeavors for all the life that I can
remember. My thinking and behavior have been molded and
shaped, both consciously and unconsciously, within a rich
and complex heritage even for many years before I was old
enough to bring to bear upon this inheritance analytical
study and reflective evaluation.

I became a Christian when I was baptized in infancy. I was
reared in a devout home where parents took seriously their
responsibility for the nurture of children in Christian faith and
living, by precept and example, and by diligent attendance
upon the ordinances of the Church. I cannot recall a time when
I did not attend public worship on Sundays, and frequently on
weekdays as well. My schooling, from the first grade through
college, was entirely in public and state institutions in Virginia
and the Carolinas. I do not remember having a single teacher
who ever openly denied or repudiated the truth of the Christian

11

religion. Many of them were very active, committed members of their respective church affiliations.

My professional education in divinity, at the University of Chicago, was oriented within a distinctly liberal and nonecclesiastical tradition that was often for me uncomfortably critical of much of the religious teaching of my earlier years. But I did not lose my faith. I changed then, as I have changed since, many particular perspectives, opinions, and tastes in regard to my Christian allegiance. Yet I have never experienced what could be called a serious revolt against "the faith of my fathers." For this good fortune, I am prepared to attribute two principal factors:

In the first place, the Methodist tradition in which I was nurtured, and the evangelical Anglicanism into which I entered during my senior year in college, were not narrowly fundamentalist, though they were both conservative and Biblically grounded. They placed primary emphasis upon the reality of religious experience rather than upon rigid norms of orthodoxy. I have never had much patience with tight little systems of propositional theology; nor have I ever found a ceremonial guidebook that I thought to be in all things correct.

In the second place, the discipline of regular attendance upon the Sacrament of Holy Communion during all the time when I was revising and reordering my convictions and values, in my divinity school years, had somehow a steadying effect that I can only call providential. I am not prepared to argue this, but only to give testimony and witness to "that which was from the beginning, which we have heard, which we have seen with our eyes, which we have looked upon and touched with our hands, concerning the word of life" (I John 1:1). In any case, the experience has left with me through all my days until the present an unshakable conviction that the liturgy is an objective instrument that God uses and through which he speaks and acts.

Such then are the personal presuppositions of our argument, presented in a selective autobiographical form. We must also say something of the primary theological orientation which we bring to our theme: namely, the gospel basis of any proper perspective upon the liturgy and its meaning in the context of Christian education.

II] WHATEVER the Church teaches about worship—or rather, whatever individual Christian teachers claim the Church teaches about worship—must necessarily be tested and judged by its conformity to the gospel, and more especially to the mind of him who as God Incarnate is himself both the object of all Christian devotion and the mediator of all Christian prayer. We cannot ignore this *test,* if we are to *testify* authentically and with conviction. Yet it is surprising and disconcerting to contemplate how frequently Christians of all traditions and persuasions do bypass this test and seek other authorities. How many pretensions, how much division among Christian people—whether they concern theological or moral, ecclesiastical or liturgical questions—would disappear if only their ordinary common sense would ask: What is the mind of Christ? What would he think or say or do in the matter?

In appealing to this test, we are not reaching back again to a Biblical fundamentalism that has shackled for centuries both Catholic and Protestant traditions, with their overly simplified but severally diverse proof-text methods. Not the gospel, nor the New Testament, nor the Bible as a whole, provides a norm for worship that can be set up canonically and rubrically. This type of literalism has played havoc among Christians. It can be illustrated from a wide range of examples—from the medieval disputes between Greeks and Latins over the use of leavened or of unleavened bread in the Eucharist, to the sabbatarian rules about Sunday observance among the Protestant sects. It has afflicted the centuries-long controversy of Anglicans and Puritans over the propriety of fixed, as over against free, prayers in public worship; of Baptists versus anti-Baptists over immersion or sprinkling. One can observe it in the "Letters to the Editor" column of our church press in much of the emotionally wrought debate about the common cup versus intinction.

"The Bible says," is an unconvincing way to begin nailing down an argument. Our ordination promise "to teach nothing, as necessary to eternal salvation, but that which you shall be persuaded may be concluded and proved by the Scripture," is no doubt a useful and salutary warning. But it does not give us a clue as to how much or how little can be so "concluded and proved." A legalistic, proof-text use of Biblical authority, whether to establish a dogma or to impose a ceremony, leaps over the centuries of history and ignores the cultural conditioning that molds all doctrinal and ritual systems. It perverts Scripture by turning it into an oracle set over and above the living tradition of the Church—that tradition which not only produced the Biblical record but provides the creative context in and through which the Word of God speaks anew and in the immediate Now.

In a study paper prepared for the Consultation on Church Unity, I have attempted to enunciate what seems to me a proper orientation toward the Scriptures which Christian educators should maintain in their approach to the meaning of liturgy and worship.[1] I repeat here the substance of those remarks:

God's people worshiped before they had a Bible. And the Biblical books are basically a record of their experience with the living God, and with his Son in the concrete person of Jesus Christ. The Scriptures "were written, edited, and canonized to be used and treasured in the context of cult and worship, and not to serve as dictionaries and encyclopedias for the reference shelves of theologians and canonists." In the apostolic age, the Church had and used, of course, an Old Testament. But it is well to remember that there had been as yet no precise agreement as to the limits of the Old Testament canon, or the relative authority of its several parts—the Law, the Prophets, and the Writings. For several generations the Church depended upon an oral testimony for its traditions of Jesus' sayings and mighty deeds. It remembered Jesus, indeed it knew him to be present, speaking and acting in the here and now by his Spirit, without recourse to authoritative written records. What it remembered was both more and less than the events and teachings of his earthly life, as these came to be recorded in the written gospels that have come down to us.[2]

From generation to generation the liturgy carries the Scriptures in a context that gives them their fullest significance and meaning. Without the living environment of worship, the Bible would be for us today a body of literature comparable to the Dead Sea Scrolls or the Hermetic writings. The Scriptures cannot be understood *religiously*—in faith—outside of the living tradition of the Church. This living tradition is handed on from age to age in the corporate

[1] This has been published in *Digest of the Proceedings of the Consultation on Church Union for 1962 and 1963,* Volumes I and II Combined. Edited by George L. Hunt, Fanwood, N.J.

[2] Cf. John Knox, *The Church and the Reality of Christ* (Harper & Row, 1962), pp. 49 ff.

worship of the Church, where the Bible is read and interpreted and its language used for the substance of prayer and praise. From this context the exegetes and theologians derive those rules and methods of interpretation that remain continuously valid and acceptable to the believing and worshipping community.

In this paper I tried to raise a question which I think is of primary importance in all ecumenical discussion—namely, how are we to decide what is meant when we say the Scriptures are a norm for testing the truth and authenticity of doctrine, ethics, or worship? An appeal to Biblical authority can be very ambiguous. The fundamentalist has a theory of literal, verbal inspiration. Yet it is notorious that these interpreters do not agree among themselves, any more than those who (like myself and my teachers) have accepted the modern, historical, critical approach to Biblical interpretation. In certain Catholic traditions, the "truth of the Bible" is interpreted according to the Church's *magisterium,* however that supreme teaching office may be institutionalized. And in some Protestant quarters we receive the impression—from their theologians, at least—that both Church and Bible are under some prior authority, whether conceived as an indefinable "Word of God" or spelled out in confessional statements of orthodoxy. Among most Anglicans, I would think, the norms of Biblical authority are derived by a subtle combination of inductive methods of historical inquiry combined with subjective evaluations of inherent rationality and moral integrity. (The great Church Father Origen, for example, applied norms of moral integrity before accepting any statement of the Bible literally; yet the Church has never had a theologian who accepted so completely and thoroughly the inspiration of the Scriptures!)

The liturgy, no less than the Scriptures, has suffered from

the imposition of theological eisegesis from without. This may well be because the liturgy is itself composed for the most part in the language of the Bible—and, like the Bible, is a primary source of doctrine according to the principle familiar in the phrase *lex orandi lex credendi*.[3] Dr. Horton Davies has reminded us how the liturgy speaks and reveals to countless worshipers a doctrine far richer than what may be encountered in the expositions of theologians. In the act of worship a congregation senses a Real Presence which its confessional theologian often denies in his systematic treatises. In prayers and hymns and chants the worshiping people discern spiritual realities that the dogmatician may rationalize out of existence.[4]

III] IT IS easy to illustrate this truth. An obvious example is the Words of Institution in the Eucharistic liturgy. Any rite of Holy Communion that includes these Words of Jesus at the Last Supper (and practically all of the liturgies in all of the Churches do contain them) can be theologically interpreted over a wide range of theories about the Real Presence of Christ in, with, or under the elements of bread and wine. The dogma of transubstantiation is imposed on the Canon of the Roman Mass no less than the memorialist or receptionist theories are imposed upon the Protestant rites. Yet in the living encounter of worship I doubt if one can really distinguish a difference in the theological commentary on these Words as contained, for example, in the hymns of Thomas Aquinas or of John Wesley, respectively.

An interesting illustration of how "canon and rubric" seek

[3] See the interesting commentary on this in Pius XII's encyclical on the liturgy, *Mediator Dei*, sections 44–47 (ed. A. Bugnini, *Documenta pontificia ad instaurationem liturgicam spectantia*, pp. 113–14.)

[4] Horton Davies, *Worship and Theology in England from Newman to Martineau, 1850–1900* (Princeton, 1962), pp. 81–85, 258–61.

fixed norms in Scripture and worship concerns the use of the
Lord's Prayer—a formulary that is more widely used by all
traditions of Christians in a greater variety of contexts of worship, both public and private, than is any other. We are not
concerned here with its variant textual tradition—the longer
Matthean and the shorter Lukan forms. Christian worshipers
have almost invariably preferred the longer Matthean version,
though most Biblical scholars consider the shorter Lukan
version more nearly authentic as *ipsissima verba* of Jesus. A
recent investigator has denied that Jesus is the author of the
prayer, and has posited a theory that Matthew composed it on
the basis of teachings and examples of prayer recorded in
Mark. The Lukan version was, in turn, an abbreviation of the
Matthean one.[5] Be all this as it may, the textual variations
themselves should warn us, at least, that we may not be dealing
with a "canon" or rule of prayer, but rather with an example
or precept of prayer that the Church felt free to adapt to its
own liturgical needs.

The gospel traditions of Jesus' delivery of the prayer are
open to different interpretations. In Matthew the prayer is
placed in a structured pattern of teaching, within the larger
frame of the "Sermon on the Mount," about almsgiving,
prayer, and fasting. The prayer serves as illustration of precepts, and is introduced by the formula "after this manner,
therefore, pray." It is clear that Matthew understood the prayer
as a model and not as a rule. In Luke, on the other hand, the
prayer is given in response to a request from one of the disciples: "Lord, teach us to pray, as John taught his disciples."
Whatever form or forms John the Baptist may have given his
followers, they seem to have observed rules of fasting and

[5] M. D. Goulder, "The Composition of the Lord's Prayer," *The
Journal of Theological Studies,* N.S. XIV (1963), 32–45.

prayer attributed to their master (cf. Luke 5:33), in the same way that Jewish rabbis gave similar injunctions to their disciples. Jesus' answer to his disciples' request is in the same tradition: "When you pray, say"—as follows. Luke's setting may therefore be taken as the delivery of a rule.

It is interesting to observe how the later liturgies interpret the tradition. In the Eastern rites, the introduction to the Lord's Prayer recalls the primary teaching of Jesus about our bold and unashamed access to God in calling him "Our Father." They make no reference to the prayer as a "canon" or rule of words. The ancient Latin bidding, which is as old as the Gregorian Sacramentary, is, to say the least, untranslatable:

Praeceptis salutaribus moniti, et divina institutione formati, audemus dicere.

Never was the legalistic language of the Latin rite more beautifully in evidence than in this introduction. Yet it does not actually say that the Lord's Prayer is anything other than what the Eastern liturgies affirm—a precept and model from the Saviour himself that encourages us to boldness and confidence in calling upon God as "Our Father."[6]

In the First Prayer Book, Archbishop Cranmer, with his characteristic habit of paraphrase in preference to literal translation, wrote: "As our Saviour Christ hath commanded and taught us, we are bold to say." This rendering was later taken into the Scottish Liturgy, and from thence it has passed to several of the current Anglican liturgies—the South African, Indian, West Indian, and Korean rites, and curiously

[6] It will be interesting to see how Roman Catholic liturgists will translate this bidding when the Mass is authorized in the various vernaculars. A recent version issued by the Dominican Fathers puts it: "Taught by thy saving precepts, and following thy divine instructions, we presume to say." This is a good try!

enough also, into the liturgy of the Church of South India. But it may be questioned whether the word *commanded* in this bidding is appropriate. There is a difference between "teach" and "command." That our Lord taught his disciples to pray after the manner of the Our Father is indisputable. But it is unlikely that he commanded them to pray exactly in this way. And if he did, the evidence does not suggest that he was delivering a liturgical formula for their corporate worship—and certainly not the kind of rattling recital of the Prayer that often characterizes Christian devotions, or, what is equally disturbing, the tendency to use the Prayer as a kind of pump to start the flow of more heartfelt communication with our Father Almighty.

2

Jesus, the Church, and the Cult

1] THE root of so much of the differences among Christians in past ages has been the assumption that our Lord Jesus Christ came into the world to found the Church—to begin a new historic religion—basically furnished with primary structures of faith, morals, ministry, and worship. This Church, it was held, though genetically continuous with Judaism, was by Jesus' intention to be stripped of the more particularistic ethnic, political, and ceremonious restrictions of Judaism, to become a universal, spiritual, and ethical community of all sorts and conditions of men who would continue the mission of Jesus, through an indeterminable period of time between his first and his Second Coming. Thus Jesus in his earthly career, amidst all the manifold revelations in teaching and deed of the universal love of God, was at the same time an Institutor of Christianity—the last, final, and perfect religion of history.

According to this view, Jesus gave the insight into the nature of God as Trinity to enrich and complete the Jewish monotheistic faith. He substituted the Golden Rule for the Jewish law of "an eye for an eye, and a tooth for a tooth" as a new code of ethical behavior. He formed the apostolate to take the place of the Jewish priesthood, establishing it as a new

hierarchy with unfailing succession. He inaugurated the sacraments, at least those of Baptism and Eucharist, to replace the
sacrificial system of the Old Testament.

There are manifold nuances of variation on this theme, that
range all the way from papal supremacy based upon the saying
to Peter in Matthew 16:16–19 to humanistic, ethical interpretations of Christianity based on the Sermon on the Mount.
This is surely the most widespread and popular conception of
Christianity as a historical phenomenon. Anglican versions of
it include the naïveté that the Church is "the extension of the
Incarnation," or the insistence upon the Quadrilateral as denoting the true and unchanging foundations of the Church.

The decisive ingredient missing in this official—and popular—conception of the Christian Church and its origin is the
dimension of the eschatological. It is the inspired contribution
of modern Biblical criticism, despite all its subjective and
negative vagaries, to have restored this cohesive principle to
our understanding of the New Testament witness. The mission
and message of Jesus were not concerned with the future
viewed as on-going history, but with the future as the fulfilling
of the present. As the Johannine evangelist puts it in the proclamation of Jesus: "The hour is coming, and now is."

Christianity is good news about *the last times*. And however
difficult it may be for Christians schooled in the traditional
and conventional patterns of thought about their historic faith
to adjust to this gospel of fulfillment—and it was just as difficult for the Jews and Gentiles to whom the gospel was first
preached—it should be the more easily understood by our
own lost generation. For we live in the nightmare of anxiety
lest tomorrow's headlines inform us that civilization is blowing
up in mushroom clouds of fire and smoke and dust.

II] JESUS CAME into the world to bring the Kingdom of God, not to establish a new or even a reformed religious institution. His mission inaugurates the end of time, when God's promises are now made manifest in fulfillment. He made no formal abolition of the Old Covenant, in whose traditions and customs and institutions he lived faithfully and without complaint. It was not necessary for him to do so, since the evident in-breaking of God's sovereign activity, as the purpose and power of his Kingdom are revealed, would bring their dissolution or their transformation in God's own appointed time. The Kingdom was both at hand and its reality had already come upon the world—most evident in the rout of Satan and the demonic powers, and in the surrender to repentance and obedience among even the publicans and sinners.

We need not concern ourselves with the question of authenticity of much of the apocalyptic frame in which Jesus' proclamation is cast—whether it belongs to his own *ipsissima verba* or is a reading back of early Christian prophetic utterance. It is not important whether Jesus envisaged any kind of interim, short or long, between his own earthly mission and the final epiphany of his glory. The interim in any case belongs not to historical time, but to eschatological time. Thus Dr. Joachim Jeremias is right in his perceptive study regarding the position of Jesus with respect to the mission to the Gentiles.[1] Jesus confines his short time to Israel, to bring to fruition Israel's destiny and calling. The coming in of the Gentiles to the true faith and obedience will be the inevitable climax of the fulfillment of Israel's vocation. It will be one of the marks of the eschatological time that follows upon this fulfillment.

Thus it was not in the purview of Jesus either to reform

[1] Joachim Jeremias, *Jesus' Promise to the Nations* (Studies in Biblical Theology No. 24; Alec R. Allenson, Inc., 1958).

Israel or to go out and form colonies of disciples among the nations. He did not prepare a new religion; he proclaimed the ultimate realization of all true religion in the absolute sovereignty of God, which is the realization at the same time of the Age to Come. It is a singular perception of the Fourth Evangelist that he sees the hardness of heart and failure of response to Jesus by the Jewish leaders in their notion that Jesus was simply a purveyor of a new sectarian teaching:

The Jews said to one another, "Where does this man intend to go that we shall not find him? Does he intend to go to the Dispersion among the Greeks and teach the Greeks? What does he mean by saying, 'You will seek me and you will not find me,' and 'Where I am you cannot come'?"   (7:35–36)

But the mission of Jesus was to fulfill his appointed role in Jerusalem, for it is in Jerusalem, not in the Dispersion, that the prophetic testimony centers in the final manifestation of the Age to Come.

Jesus made no deliberate separation of himself from the people of God. He proclaimed no new creed. He accepted without question the summation of the Law and the Prophets in the daily confession of the *Shema,* which he doubtless recited with other devout Jews of his generation:

Hear, O Israel; the Lord our God is one Lord. And thou shalt love the Lord thy God with all thy heart, and with all thy soul, and with all thy mind, and with all thy strength.   (Deut. 6:4; Mark 12:30)

His whole life and ministry fulfilled the injunction with which the *Shema* was given: "These words, which I command thee this day, shall be in thine heart: and thou shalt teach them diligently . . . and shalt talk of them . . . and shalt bind them for a sign" (Deut. 6:6 ff.).

The question of Jesus' own Messianic consciousness has

been a conundrum for devout students of the gospels. No
solution of the problem seems as yet to command general
assent. Let us say simply this: In the appropriate time and
place Jesus was not reticent about the uniqueness of his Person—whether he viewed himself as Messiah or Son of Man
or Son of God. He did not reject the confession and reverence
of men. But it is equally true that he formulated no creed
about his Person as a condition of discipleship; and again and
again he redirected the acclaim and compliments offered to
himself to a gratitude and faith and obedience toward God.

If Jesus had been a reformer of religion, and of the Jewish
religion in particular, we might have expected from him, if
not a new creed, at least a new code. But the "new commandment" of his ethical teaching is only the positive implementa-
tion and fulfillment of the old commandments as they are
given unity and cohesion and consistency in the love of neighbor. The Law of Love, being a creative principle of life, is not
capable of statutory regulation or of detailed systematization.
Its application differs in every situation of personal relationships. When the tempting lawyer asked Jesus to define "neighbor," he received not a definition but the story of a single
instance of a neighbor's behavior.

Certainly there can be no dispute that in Jesus' teaching
there is nothing comparable to a sectarian code of ethics.
Every attempt of later ages to reduce his principles to such a
code is shattered by the constant necessity of exceptions, or at
best an involved method of casuistry.[2] If there is any definitive
and irrefutable answer to the hypotheses purveyed in cheap

[2] Episcopalians should know this, having agonized for years about
the so-called Marriage Canon, in which they had made difficulties for
themselves by attempting to erect a precept of Jesus into a strictly
defined law of human relationships.

paperback pronouncements that endeavor to explain the origins of Christianity on the basis of the Qumran community documents, it can be found in a comparison of the Essene ethic with that of the gospel. It is simply inconceivable to think of Jesus excluding sinners—even apostates—from the outreach of love and mercy and hope of forgiveness and participation in the covenanted promises of God's Age that is coming.

A favored interpretation of all Catholic exegesis has fastened upon the institution of the apostolate as a fundamental plan of Jesus for the continuation of his mission. Yet it can only be maintained by ignoring the fact that this institution belongs, in the gospel tradition, entirely to the post-Resurrection revelation. During his earthly ministry Jesus selected the Twelve, representative as they were in number of the whole historic community of Israel, to be his assistants in the immediate proclamation of the coming of the Kingdom, and his assessors in the final judgment that was impending. They were not sent out into all the world, but into the towns and villages of the "lost sheep" of Israel. He did not initiate them into the program of a "coming great Church" but into the mysteries of the Kingdom of God.

The single exception one might proffer to this pre-Resurrection formation of the Twelve is the much-disputed and belabored saying to Peter in Matthew 16:16–19. It is unfortunate that ecclesiastical controversy has clouded all efforts to be objective in interpreting this pericope. But if it is understood eschatologically, and not institutionally, it makes very good sense and requires no apodictic refutation of its authenticity. Whatever it may mean regarding the relation of Peter to the rest of the Twelve, it belongs incontestably to the other traditions of Jesus' sayings concerning the role of the Twelve with him in the coming crisis of the establishment of the Kingdom,

when they shall sit with him on thrones judging the twelve
tribes (cf. Matt. 19:28; Luke 22:30). With him they shall
share the "power of the keys" in the manifestation and revelation of the elect, the true "church" and people of God. This
eschatological promise is transformed by the Johannine evangelist, in a *post*-Resurrection scene, into an ecclesiastical authorization of Spirit-endowment to give or to withhold abso-
lution.

III] THE outlook and intentions of Jesus regarding the
end-time are most clearly indicated in his attitude and relation to the Jewish cult. Again, it is not a matter of any formal
abrogation or rejection of the Old Testament system, but a
promise of the fulfillment of that to which it ultimately points—
an inner obedience of the heart to the love of God and of
neighbor. He did not attack the Sabbath or the ritual and
ceremonial laws of cleanness and uncleanness, but only those
interpretations of them that made them ends rather than means
of man's wholeness of person and relationships. If a man's love
for his animal prompts him instinctively to save the beast that
has accidentally fallen into a well on the Sabbath day, how
much more should a man take occasion immediately, whether
it be the Sabbath day or not, to heal his unfortunate fellow man
(cf. Luke 14:5).

For Jesus, all cultic demands must be subservient to human
need, whether physical or spiritual, and to interpersonal reconciliation. A sacrificial offering is worthless if the offerer is
conscious of enmity or of unresolved obligation to his neighbor
(cf. Matt. 5:23–24). In this attitude, Jesus was not an inno-
vator but stood within the best tradition of prophetic and
rabbinic teaching.

Much has been made of the fact that the gospels never

portray Jesus in a formal act of sacrifice in the Temple. Yet
he never said that his disciples should not offer sacrifices, and
—assuming for the moment that the Last Supper was a Passover meal—he made arrangements for his disciples to prepare
what was necessary for the feast. It is probable that Jesus pre-
dicted the destruction of the Temple, but the witnesses brought
in against him at his trial could not agree as to the precise way
he envisaged it. This is doubtless because Jesus foresaw the end
of the Temple eschatologically, its historic purpose coming to
fulfillment as "a house of prayer for all people" in the Age to
Come. Thus the cleansing of the Temple was prophetic of its
transformation to the ends of God's ultimate purpose. It is
not likely that Jesus had in view the precise kind of destruction
that overcame the Temple historically in the climax of the
Jewish rebellion against Rome (A.D. 70). Later Christian re-
flection upon that event has colored the tradition of Jesus'
prophetic insight, and so we have been left with the ambigui-
ties of the gospel records.

Jesus did not provide, in any case, a new rite and cultus
to replace that of the Temple. However, we have inherited an
ecclesiastical tradition, if not dogma, that maintains that Jesus
instituted at least the two sacraments of Baptism and Eucharist. Supposedly, these two sacraments were to replace the old
Jewish cultus, not to be added alongside it; and to Jesus is
attributed the institution of their essential form and matter.

To question this universal tradition of the Church, whether
Catholic or Protestant, respecting the "dominical institution"
of the sacraments is hazardous. Let us say at once that we do
not deny for a moment that the two sacraments of Baptism
and Eucharist have a firm basis in what Jesus himself experienced and did. That he was himself baptized at the hands of
John the Baptist, and in that experience received a vivid con-

sciousness of his unique relation to God the Father and endowment by the Holy Spirit, can no more be arbitrarily read out of the record than that he broke bread and shared a cup with his disciples in the upper room in Jerusalem on the night in which he was betrayed. What is essentially in question is whether Jesus at any time during his earthly—that is, pre-Resurrection—life and ministry formally instituted these rites for the future constitution of a community of his disciples after his death.

Almost every student who accepts critical methods of Biblical interpretation has virtually abandoned the notion of a "dominical institution" of Baptism in its classical reference to the Great Commission of Matthew's Resurrection narrative (28:19). This is due not merely to a suspicion that the Trinitarian formula there given represents a "reading back" into the Resurrection tradition of later church usage. It is simply impossible to make sense of the struggle that developed in the apostolic Church over the Gentile mission, if the disciples had received so clear-cut a directive to evangelize "all nations" in this manner. Otherwise than in this commission at the end of Matthew, the Synoptic Gospels betray not the slightest concern on the part of Jesus about a rite of baptism, even though they preserve the most complimentary testimony of Jesus to the person and mission of John the Baptist. In the Synoptics, when Jesus speaks of Baptism, he refers to his death —to the ultimate tribulation and surrender of life that the coming of the final age will or may demand. And when he uses the word *regeneration* (Matt. 19:28, KJ), he refers to the Age to Come, not to a sacramental experience (as it is used, for example, in Titus 3:5).

We should be wary also of misuse of the pericope concerning Jesus' receiving and blessing little children, as though it were a lesson proving the legitimacy of baptizing infants. It may well be, as Professor Oscar Cullmann and others have attempted to prove, that the pericope as we have it shows traces of a baptismal liturgy of the early Church.[3] But the point of this particular tradition is not that Jesus explicitly authorizes a rite of baptism administered to infants. It is simply another illustration of the absolute openness of God's love and of his Kingdom to all sorts and conditions of men.

The insistence of the majority of Christians in later ages upon the appropriateness of baptizing infants cannot be defended by using this pericope as any canonical institution. But it can be definitively supported by a prior and more legitimate query of the "mind of Christ." Can we possibly imagine that our Lord would have excluded infants from participation in the redeemed community of the world to come? The answer to this question is certainly No. If the Church on earth is in any sense an earnest of the eschatological Kingdom, the communion of the Church must be open to every age and condition of man—and this includes infants and imbeciles and all unfortunates and limited people, no less than intelligent or consciously committed adults.

The evidence of the Johannine gospel concerning Baptism is admittedly disputable and ambiguous. Devout exegetes of this gospel seem divided between the sacramentarians and the antisacramentarians. Our difficulties stem, of course, from the subtlety of the evangelist in weaving together several facets of meaning in all his material. He makes no explicit statement that Jesus was himself baptized by John, yet we cannot escape

[3] Oscar Cullmann, *Baptism in the New Testament* (Studies in Biblical Theology No. 1; Henry Regnery Co., 1950), pp. 71–80. But *contra,* see Kurt Aland, *Did the Early Church Baptize Infants?* (Westminster Press, 1963), p. 96.

the conviction that the evangelist knew this tradition very well (cf. John 1:32–33 with Mark 1:10). Similarly, he alone provides no narrative of the institution of the Eucharist, yet he gives more attention to the Last Supper than do the Synoptic evangelists. He tells us specifically (or at least his editor does, 4:2) that Jesus' disciples baptized, apparently with his permission if not express authorization, but that Jesus himself did not baptize.

More crucial is the conversation with Nicodemus: "Unless one is born of water and the Spirit, he cannot enter the kingdom of God" (3:5). We know that certain ancient texts omit the reference to water, albeit most modern critics do not accept this omission as a correct reading. If we look at the pericope in its total context, however, it seems clear that Jesus' pronouncements to the learned rabbi are eschatological and not institutional. Jesus is concerned with the new birth, Spirit-birth, "from above," and the conversation is set in a large frame of contextual reference that contrasts this new Spirit-birth with the purifyings of the Jews, and indeed of John the Baptist himself. It is not a very secure foundation to use the passing reference to "water" in the dialogue with Nicodemus as a "dominical institution" of Baptism.

With respect to the Eucharist, we are hung upon the dilemma of both the authenticity and the meaning of the command: "Do this in remembrance of me." In our two oldest traditions of the Supper—each of them independent of the other—Paul refers to the command (I Cor. 11:24–25), Mark does not. The evidence of Luke is textually disputed. But if Dr. Jeremias' interpretation of the command is right[4]—and I

---

[4] Joachim Jeremias, *The Eucharistic Words of Jesus* (Macmillan, 1955), pp. 159–65.

have not seen as yet any definitive refutation of it[5]—it does not refer to a rite to be continued by the disciples for their own recalling of Jesus during the interim that awaits his Second Coming. It refers rather to the impending eschatological conflict into the climactic stage of which Jesus was then entering. Thus he summons his disciples to remember him before God in this ultimate test. This interpretation is entirely in harmony with the other sayings of Jesus at the Supper, and particularly the so-called "vow of abstinence." This Supper is the last time Jesus will eat and drink with his disciples in the dimensions of this earthly life and age. The next time he shares the meal with them, it will be in the Kingdom of God.

How long will that be? I do not think that Jesus in that hour would be concerned with "the times or seasons" of what God had fixed by his own authority (cf. Acts 1:7). For in a very real sense, he was passing out of the realm of times and seasons. The Supper was the earnest of what is now and about to be fulfilled. Its next celebration would be the Messianic banquet.

It is probably unlikely that we shall ever resolve the disputed question of the specific cultic occasion of the Last Supper—whether it was a Passover meal or merely an ordinary meal of a Jewish company of friends.[6] In either case, the old order has come to an end.

> Types and shadows have their ending,
> For the newer rite is here . . .

[5] See A. J. B. Higgins, *The Lord's Supper in the New Testament* (Studies in Biblical Theology No. 6; SCM Press Ltd., 1952), p. 55, who refers to an article in Dutch by W. C. van Unnik, which I have not seen. See also H. Kosmala, " 'Das tut zu meinem Gedächtnis,' " *Novum Testamentum* IV (1961), 81–94.

[6] I have given my own views in an article, "Are Both the Synoptics and John Correct about the Date of Jesus' Death?" *Journal of Biblical Literature* LXXX (1961), 123–32.

But the "newer rite" is not a substitution or even a transformation of the older rite, but its fulfillment—and a fulfillment in
perhaps a deeper sense than St. Thomas Aquinas imagined
when he appended to this cited couplet another:

> Faith, our outward sense befriending,
> Makes our inward vision clear.

IV] IN PRESENTING Jesus as a thorough-going eschatolo-
gist (not apocalyptist, be it noted), we believe a consistent
principle can be given to the saving record and tradition of the
gospel. This principle, or theory, is a modern one and is not
by any means completely established by criticism, much less
acknowledged by most Christians. It is possible to propose
texts that give a different orientation to the tradition. But this
is so because the gospels are not biographical documents, but
church texts. It is admitted on all sides that they reflect much
of the life and concerns of the early Christian movement in the
apostolic age. We believe, however, that the other New Testament writings give a consistent testimony to the fact, which we
have tried to expound, that in Jesus' life, teaching, mission,
and death, liturgy considered as cultic observance based upon
legalistic and canonical regulation, reaches a denouement that
is not so much abolition or abrogation as it is fulfillment.

The hour is coming when neither on this mountain nor in Jerusalem will you worship the Father. . . . But the hour is coming, and
now is, when the true worshipers will worship the Father in spirit
and truth, for such the Father seeks to worship him.

(JOHN 4:21, 23)

The decisive seal of this transformation is surely the final
and perfect oblation of Jesus that fulfills all sacrifice, and the
act of God in raising him from the dead that inaugurates, as

a first fruit, the glory that is to be revealed. Alfred Loisy's famous and oft-quoted quip that Jesus came to bring the Kingdom, but what came was the Catholic Church, suffers from the distortions of all epigrams. But it contains the root of the matter. The Resurrection changed everything; even though it took a generation for the disciples to comprehend its shattering significance—if indeed the Church has ever fully comprehended its implications.

To state the matter bluntly, the mission and triumph of Jesus dissolved the line of demarcation that separates the sacred from the profane, and the cultic sphere of religion from its witness and daily service in the world. For it has sanctified the totality of creation, and inaugurated its liberation from the bondage of futility and decay that it might obtain "the glorious liberty of the children of God" (cf. Rom. 8:20–21).

Whatever cult or cultus the Church has developed for the promotion and edification of its own corporate life of worship, witness, and service, has to be understood by reference to an otherworldly, eschatological fulfillment to which it points. Baptism is more than an initiation ceremony into a historic community. It is death and resurrection. Sunday is more than a cultic holy day set aside for special religious observance. It is a reminder of the ultimate Day of the Lord when there shall be neither day nor night, weeks, months, nor years. And the Eucharist is more than an esoteric communion in consecrated elements known only to the band of initiated mystagogues. It is the sanctification of every table that is spread in loving generosity and selfless surrender to the need of the hungry, and at the same time a tasting of the powers of the Age to Come.

3

The Christian Abolition
of Cult

1] THE meager notices of the primitive Church in Jerusalem, contained in the first few chapters of the Book of Acts,
are the despair of critical historians. All that they tell us could
have happened within a few weeks, if not a few days; yet the
evangelist gives an impression to the reader of a gradual
evolvement of the Church's mission to the world that might
have extended over almost a decade.

Some of the traditions of Acts appear repetitious, some of
them suspiciously legendary; and in the absence of other docu-
mentary materials from the same period, it is difficult to
separate authentic facts from the evangelist's interpretations.
It is not that "Luke" manipulates his sources; rather he has
been selective of those events and circumstances that fit pro-
portionately into his broader vision of how the gospel passed
from Jerusalem to Rome, from Judaism to the Gentile world,
in response to the Resurrection commission. Acts is a gospel,
no less than a history; and it is a consummate work of literary
art, as it is of kerygmatic edification.[1]

Certain characteristics of the primitive community of dis-

[1] See the perceptive study of W. C. van Unnik, "The 'Book of
Acts' the Confirmation of the Gospel," *Novum Testamentum* IV
(1960), 26–59.

ciples and believers stand out, however, with utmost clarity—characteristics that fundamentally document and support our contention that Jesus did not intend to found a new religion, but to bring the old one to fulfillment. Professor Eduard Schweizer has summarized the situation in this way:

. . . the primitive Church continued in its Jewish national and religious associations—this means that it regarded as valid the priesthood, the sacrificial system, the synagogue services, and the law. The kingdom of God remained in the future, and it was not for them to bring it in by reforms. All Israel, not just one severed group, was called to God's kingdom. Thus continuity between Israel and the open circle of Jesus' disciples was preserved; they were still a band of messengers.[2]

Professor Schweizer goes on to point out how different this conception of itself by the primitive Church was from the Qumran group, for example. The latter regarded itself as a "nucleus" around which the rest of Israel would be gathered at the day of salvation. But such a view was impossible to the early disciples of the apostolic Church:

It cannot, as a better nucleus with a higher status, separate itself from the "fringe members"; nor can it still regard as the real Israel, even for the coming time of salvation, the Israel that rejected Jesus and his call to repentance.[3]

We might say that the disciples formed a "Way"—among many other "ways"—within Israel, but a Way that was open ended. Just as the mission of Jesus, so its own witness and proclamation were open to whosoever would call upon the Name of the Lord. It continues fully in the corporate life of

[2] *Church Order in the New Testament* (Studies in Biblical Theology No. 32; Alec R. Allenson, Inc., 1961), pp. 34–35.
[3] *Ibid.*, p. 36.

Judaism, yet with a crucial distinction. It is already living *there* where the promises to Judaism had been pointing, in the Spirit-filled life of the in-breaking Age to Come. It has, to be sure, the germ of a creed: "This Jesus whom you crucified, God has made both Lord and Christ" (Acts 2:36). It has the root of a new ethical principle—at least, the wall between the strict Hebraist Jew and the lax Hellenizing Jew is cracking. It has a hierarchy of its own—the leadership of witness, teaching, and prayer of the apostles. It has a cult: the "breaking of bread" in their houses.

Is it really a cult—in the sense of the term as understood by a Jew or a pagan? There is no holy place; there are no sacred times and seasons. The domestic gatherings for the breaking of bread defy all attempts to distinguish them as sacral meals or as partially sacral meals combined with ordinary meals. The Church can meet at any time and in any available place. It has no priesthood in the commonly accepted sense. Indeed, never in the New Testament is any individual Christian separated in status from his fellow believers by the dignity and sacral appel-lation of "priest." Priesthood belongs to Christ, and in and through him to the whole body of believers.

It is true, there is a summons to Baptism, a baptism that is no more cultic and exclusive than was John's. For the gift of the Spirit, the distinguishing characteristic of Christian Bap-tism, is associated by no means necessarily with the perform-ance of the water ceremony. It comes before, during, and after the rite. The Book of Acts is notoriously loose about this, as compared with later treatises on the sacraments. And St. Paul, who had a far more profound theology of Baptism than did the author of Acts, presents us at the same time with a para-doxical note that he did not consider the administration of Baptism an important part of his apostolic ministry. This in-

deed is a strange and thought-provoking commentary upon the
Great Commission at the end of Matthew!

Of course, differentiations looking toward cultic observance
began at a very early time to emerge, and became the more
clear once the separation of the disciples from Judaism took
place. The exact time or occasion of this separation cannot
be pinpointed. I suspect it first occurred in Antioch, when the
disciples were first called—or first called themselves—Christians (Acts 11:26).[4] The hard-fought decision over the admission of Gentiles to full fellowship, without necessity of ad-
herence to Jewish cult, was no doubt the primary seal upon
the separation. So far as the outside world was concerned, we
have no evidence that the separation was clearly evident before the time of Nero. And perhaps it says something about
the ambivalent nature of Christianity as a *religio* in the classical sense that the Roman government never proscribed it as
such in a precise edict, but satisfied itself in taking police
measures under the discretion given to magistrates in dealing
with those accused of it as "Christians."[5] The Roman State
was never quite certain whether Christianity was a religious
heresy or a political "fifth column"—with much the same con-

[4] I have prepared a study of this, "The Occasion of the Initial
Break between Judaism and Christianity," soon to appear in the *Wolf-
son Jubilee Volumes,* to be published by the American Academy for
Jewish Research.

[5] This view of the legal basis of the "persecutions" seems now to
be well established. See the comments of J. Vogt and H. Last in their
respective articles "Christenverfolgung," *Reallexikon für Antike und
Christentum,* I, 1159–1228; also J. W. Ph. Borleffs, "Institutum Ne-
ronianum," *Vigiliae Christianae* VI (1952), 129–45; A. N. Sherwin-
White, "The Early Persecutions and Roman Law Again," *The Journal
of Theological Studies,* N. S. III (1952), 199–213; and J. Moreau, *Die
Christenverfolgung im römischen Reich* (Berlin, 1961).

fusion that many Christians today look upon the threat of Communism.

II] THE New Testament testifies to, without documenting, the separation of Christian believers into conventicles disassociated from Judaism. In this emergence of a new "religion" there are established cultic patterns—Baptism and laying on of hands, Lord's Supper or Eucharist, Sunday as a weekly time of meeting (without prejudice to gatherings on other days), liturgical forms of praise and prayer, preaching, and all the rest.

Yet it is important to note that the New Testament has no vocabulary of cult. Where it uses cultic terms, derived either from Judaism or the pagan world, it uses them indiscriminately of worship and of service in the world. More often than not such words are applied to the redemptive work of Jesus, and then by reference to him to the whole life of Christians. Our English word *service* exactly translates the ambivalence of the New Testament cultic terminology.

We know, for example, that St. Paul did not use the word *liturgy* and its cognates in the strictly cultic sense of his Old Testament Bible, the Septuagint. He employed it of his own apostolic ministry (Rom. 15:16) and of the vocation in the world of its rulers and "powers that be" (Rom. 13:6). He used sacrificial terms of Christ (Rom. 3:24–25; I Cor. 5:7) and of the entire life and witness of Christian obedience (Rom. 12:1; Phil. 4:18). In his directives to the Corinthians about the Eucharist and their abuses of its proper observance (I Cor. 11:17 ff.), we cannot determine whether he uses "Lord's Supper" to describe the entire gathering for common worship, edification, and charity, or would limit it to specific cultic formularies and ceremonies that took place at the gathering.

Likewise, when he accuses the Corinthians of not "discerning the Lord's body," it is more likely that he refers to the Church than that he denotes the sacramental species.

What is true of St. Paul is true of other writers of letters and treatises in the New Testament. First Peter is often described as a baptismal homily set forth in the form of a letter. Professor F. L. Cross has offered the hypothesis that it is actually a baptismal liturgy.[6] But the theological and the ethical, the cultic and the profane vocabulary of the epistle are so interwoven that one cannot separate the strands. The priestly, sacrificial language of Chapter 2, especially, describes the totality of Christian existence; and the "spiritual sacrifices acceptable to God through Jesus Christ" (verse 5), in particular, cannot be properly interpreted as referring to the Eucharist alone. The whole context links, in a single whole, worship and witness, liturgy and mission, of those who are "God's own people," that they might "declare the wonderful deeds of him who called you out of darkness into his marvelous light." St. Peter uses ἐξαγγείλητε of "declaring" or "proclaiming" in the same way that St. Paul uses its cognate καταγγέλλετε of "proclaiming the Lord's death" in the celebration of the Lord's Supper.

One could make the same examination with the same results in the treatise called the Epistle to the Hebrews. Despite its elaborate cultic terminology, the treatise is a veritable charter document of the consummation of all cult in the sacrificial

---

[6] *I. Peter, A Paschal Liturgy* (A. R. Mowbray and Co., Ltd., 1954); see also M. E. Boismard, "Une liturgie baptismale dans la Prima Petri," *Revue Biblique* LXIII (1956), 182–208; but *contra*, see C. F. D. Moule, "The Nature and Purpose of I Peter," *New Testament Studies* III (1956), 1–11; and T. C. G. Thornton, "I Peter, A Paschal Liturgy?" *The Journal of Theological Studies,* N. S. XII (1961), 14–26.

offering of Christ. It is curious that later ages have fastened upon this epistle for the application of cultic vocabulary to the Eucharist, and the more unfortunately for much of our popular hymnody about the Eucharist. But the author in no place speaks of Christ as a "Victim" in the Sacrament, or of his making a perpetual "offering" of himself upon an "altar" in heaven. He made his offering once for all upon the Cross, and his ministry in heaven is intercessory.[7]

In this connection, attention should be called to the acute study of that *crux* of interpreters of Hebrews 13:9–14, which was recently published by Professor Helmut Koester. He points out that "the sacrifice 'outside the camp' puts an end to all cultic and sacred performances, and those who have this 'altar' are not to dwell in sacred places and to deal with ritual regulations, but to go out into the world to bear his reproach."[8] Dr. Koester denies that the author opposes sacraments. He is challenging sacramentalism, a doctrine of "direct communion with the divine in the sacrament or in any other regulations and rituals," as over against an acceptance of the challenges and sufferings of human existence in its secular reality. For such teaching "failed to acknowledge the paradoxical character of the divine presence in the salvation focused in the cross of Calvary 'outside the camp,' and did not see the involvement of the Christian existence in the non-sacred character of this life as a necessary consequence from the 'unholy sacrifice' of Jesus, upon which the Christian faith rests."[9]

We shall not belabor the point further. A supporting treat-

[7] See the study of W. Stott, "The Conception of 'Offering' in the Epistle to the Hebrews," *New Testament Studies* IX (1962), 62–67.

[8] " '*Outside the Camp*': Hebrews 13.9–14," *The Harvard Theological Review* LV (1962), p. 313.

[9] *Ibid.,* p. 315.

ment may be found in the essays on worship of our North American Commission on Faith and Order—the partial fruit of some eight years of study and discussion by representatives of Orthodox, Lutheran, Anglican, Reformed, Methodist, and Congregationalist traditions.[10] Put in its baldest form, the thesis was thus stated by Dean Alexander Schmemann of St. Vladimir's Seminary, who said that the Christian transformation of Jewish cult consisted

in the abolishment of cult as such, or at least in the complete destruction of the old philosophy of cult. The Christian *leitourgia* is not a "cult" if by this term we mean a sacred action, or rite, performed in order to establish "contact" between the community and God, whatever the meaning and the nature of such contact. A "cult" by its very essence presupposes a radical distinction between the "sacred" and the "profane," and, being a means of reaching or expressing the "sacred," it posits all the non-sacred as "profane."[11]

Dean Schmemann goes on to say, in words that all of us on the Commission would heartily endorse:

From this point of view the Christian *leitourgia* did not originate as a cult. It was not a cult, because within the *ecclesia*—the royal priesthood, the holy people, the peculiar nation—the distinction between the sacred and the profane, which is the very condition of cult, has been abolished. The Church is not a natural community which is "sanctified" through the cult. In its essence the Church is the presence, the actualization in this world of the "world to come," in this *aeon*—of the Kingdom.[12]

This is very strong medicine indeed, coming as it does from a theologian of the Orthodox Church—a Church which we

[10] Massey H. Shepherd, Jr. (ed.), *Worship in Scripture and Tradition* (Oxford, 1963).

[11] *Ibid.,* p. 172.

[12] *Ibid.,* p. 173.

commonly think of as cultic par excellence. It fits no less with the quite independent study of one of our Anglican commissioners, Professor Franklin W. Young, who noted that New Testament scholarship today underscores the fact that the traditional terminology of cult—*latreia, leitourgia, diakonia,* etc.—is not employed in the New Testament writings in reference to cultic worship, and for a good reason:

... the Church's conviction that, even as God's holy place of meeting men was disclosed in Jesus Christ, so Jesus Christ's action was determinative for the meaning of worship. ... In the cultic sense the early Christians had nothing to do to worship. Unlike the Jews with their cultic service (*latreia, leitourgia*) well defined by Torah, the Christians had none. What they were to do in response to God, Christ had done. Or to put it another way: the true worship of God was disclosed in Christ's action. Their attention was focused on Christ's service.[13]

[13] *Ibid.,* pp. 89–90.

4

Liturgy or Cult: Source
or Resource?

1] THE New Testament perspective upon liturgy and
worship persisted throughout the patristic age. If we may cite
Dean Schmemann again, "The Fathers do not 'reflect' on
liturgy. For them it is not an *object* of theological inquiry and
definition, but rather the living source and the ultimate cri-
terion of all Christian thought."[1] It is worth noting that there
exist no treatises on "liturgics" as such from the patristic
period. There are works on prayer and the spiritual life, and
catechetical instructions on the sacraments delivered to the
newly baptized. These have to do with the normal and necessary pastoral ministry of the Church. But the liturgy viewed
as a definable, distinct category of religious phenomena is
absent from the purview of the ancient Fathers.

One might bring forward as exceptions the "customaries"
of the early Church, the documents known as Church Orders,
beginning with the *Didache* and Hippolytus' *Apostolic Tradition.* These were manuals that covered the whole range of what
we would today call "practical theology." But their purpose
was certainly not to isolate the liturgy from the more ordinary,
or as we should say "secular," round of daily Christian living,

1 *Worship in Scripture and Tradition,* p. 167.

but to direct the totality of Christian life in ways of sound tradition.

It is well-known how difficult it is for scholars to decide whether the thanksgivings before and after meals in the *Didache* (chaps. ix–x) refer to the Eucharistic sacrament or to the Agape fellowship meal. In the unmistakable reference to the Eucharist (chap. xiv) as "a pure sacrifice," the author or compiler does not refer to the nature of the bread that is broken or to the ritual of thanksgiving that is offered, but to the reconciliation of the worshipers who participate. It is the love and forgiveness of Christian brothers that assure that "the sacrifice is not profaned" (literally, "made common"), and so is fulfilled the prophecy that "in every place and time a pure sacrifice shall be offered unto me, for I am a great King, says the Lord, and my Name is wonderful among the peoples" (Mal. 1:11, 14).

In Hippolytus' treatise there is certainly a clearer distinction between the Eucharist and the Agape, not only in the manner of celebration, but in their respective obligatory or voluntary character. Yet Hippolytus uses the Pauline phrase "the Lord's Supper" to denote the Agape (chap. xxvi)! He insists that the unbaptized are not to participate in the table grace of the Agape, but to have their separate thanksgiving. This injunction reveals in particular the difference in outlook of the ancient Church from that of the Church today. In the ancient Church the real dividing line between the realm of redemption and the realm yet to be redeemed was Baptism, not a disciplinary admission to communicant—that is, cultic—status.

Churchmen today would be horrified at the thought that unbaptized persons should not be permitted to eat at the same table and share the same table grace at our ordinary church suppers. We even welcome them to participate in the Church's public prayers; though, of course, we exclude them, along with our own baptized but unconfirmed children, from receiving Communion. Otherwise we let them share in all the benefits and blessings of the rest of our rites. Such a practice would have been inconceivable in the patristic Church, which allowed the unbaptized to be present only at the readings of the Scriptures and the sermon—the kerygmatic and missionary introduction of the liturgy. Before any prayer was offered they were dismissed.

I do not believe that the original motivation of this practice was due to any cultic distinction of the sacred and the profane, though it may have entered into consideration in the later patristic age. It was due rather to the clear conviction of the early Church that the baptized had entered into another realm of existence—the Age to Come. They took the prayers of the liturgy with utmost realism, and with a sense of their corporate force, that startles the pervasive individualistic thinking of our times. That is to say, they considered it impossible for one who had not professed Christ to participate in prayer in his Name; and one could not merely be present and watch the proceedings. For only those with faith really knew what was taking place. They did not consider the liturgy a means of instruction.

The same thinking lies behind the universal custom of the ancient Church, even after the cultic sense of liturgy began to take hold, of never explaining the meaning of the sacramental mysteries during the preparation of the catechumens. All the patristic lectures on the sacraments—the so-called "mystagogical lectures"—were delivered to the new converts *after* and not before they were initiated at the Easter rites.[2]

[2] We possess such courses of lectures from Cyril of Jerusalem, Theodore of Mopsuestia, John Chrysostom, and Ambrose.

This again would seem foolish to our modern ways of thinking and doing. Not many clergy today would risk withholding instruction on the meaning of Baptism, Confirmation, and Eucharist until after the class of candidates had participated in them. But then, the early Church did not understand the liturgy as an object of knowledge but as a subject of experience. One could not understand what one had not experienced, no matter how many lectures were given and instructional exercises imposed. The liturgy can only be known from the inside, since it is the very frame of the new total existence with Christ "in the heavenly places" (Eph. 1:3, 20).

The ancient Church did not practice the so-called *disciplina arcana* because of a fear of profaning what was sacred. In fact, apologetic writers were quite prepared to describe Christian worship to pagan readers, with a view toward showing its ethical and spiritual character. They were reticent simply for the reason—so often given by Origen, for example, in his sermons—that the unbaptized would not really know what they were talking about.[3] The liturgy is a mystery known only to the faithful in this sense. It is not a secret, like the cults of the mystery-religions. It is a new order of eschatological existence, which those still living in the old *aeon* cannot possibly comprehend, until they have died and been raised to newness of life in Christ.

Another passage in Hippolytus is apropos of our point—

[3] On the *disciplina arcana,* see the bibliography listed in E. Bourque, *Étude sur les sacramentaires romains,* I (Studi di antichità cristiana XX; Rome, 1948), p. 1, to which may be added P. Batiffol's article "Arcane," *Dictionnaire de théologie catholique,* I, 1738–58. I find myself in agreement with Abbé Bourque that recent discoveries have demonstrated how restricted was the "field of the law of the arcana."

namely, the well-known reference, first of its kind, to "fasting communion" (chap. xxxii) :

Let every one of the faithful be careful to partake of the Eucharist before he eats anything else. For if he partakes with faith, even though some deadly thing were given him, after this it cannot hurt him.

The injunction occurs with directions about the daily reception of the Sacrament by the laity from consecrated bread taken home from church—a custom that obtained in North Africa and possibly also in Rome (if Hippolytus is really Roman) during the third century. This practice would shock churchmen today, who would consider it very remiss for the laity to possess the reserved Sacrament and communicate themselves from it. We will not even allow laymen to administer Communion in church under the eye and supervision of the clergy. Is this itself an indication of how we have, apart from all canonical questions of appropriate discipline, clericalized and sacralized the Sacrament?

Be that as it may, Hippolytus' directive does suggest that he views the consecrated Eucharist as a kind of *sacrum,* at least when it is received in faith. But one should note carefully the reason he gives for receiving the Eucharist each day before taking other food. It is not a cultic reason—such as one usually hears today in defense of "fasting communion," namely, that it is an act of honor to our Lord to receive his Body and Blood before we have "profaned" our stomachs with other food—from God's good creation. Hippolytus is not interested in the honor of the Sacrament but in the wholeness of the believer. The Eucharist sanctified the recipient so that no "deadly thing" (*mortale quodcumque*) could harm him. By deadly thing he is obviously thinking of anything that might happen to a Christian to bring about not only physical but also spiritual death. The point is not so much the sacrosanctness of the Eucharistic species, though that is implied, but the sacredness of the total daily life of the Christian in what our Prayer Book calls "all the changes and chances of this mortal life."

II] IT IS not possible to point to any exact time or occasion when the Church began to look upon the liturgy as a cult. That it should come to do so was no doubt inevitable, once it recognized and accepted the fact that sin exists in the fellowship of believers no less than in the world outside, that the Church is a mixed society of wheat and tares that will not be finally separated until the Last Judgment. Thus, for example, we understand the gradual shift in meaning of such a word as *saint* from a definition of each and every baptized person to a specialized connotation of the more distinguished witnesses to the Faith. Thus in the Creed, there is an ambiguity in the phrase "The Communion of Saints"—whether "saints" refers to persons or to things, to the whole community of the redeemed, or to the holy and sacral mysteries and actions in which the redeemed are privileged to share.[4]

---

[4] The traditional view that "Communion of Saints" refers to persons is ably supported by J. N. D. Kelly, *Early Christian Creeds* (Longmans, Green and Co., 1950), pp. 388–97. For the opposite view—that it refers to the sacraments—see the dissertation of Istvan Benkö (who follows his teacher Oscar Cullmann), *Sanctorum communio* (Basel, 1951), and my review of this work in *Review of Religion* XIX (1955), 212–14. A good illustration of our point is the way the medieval Church misunderstood the primary meaning of the Festival of All Saints, and followed it by the institution of "All Souls." But, as the late Professor B. S. Easton said so aptly, "in Anglican tradition 'All Saints' is 'All Souls' as well; this accords better with the New Testament doctrine of 'sainthood.' " B. S. Easton and H. C. Robbins, *The Eternal Word in the Modern World* (Scribners, 1937), p. 297.

It is perhaps unfair to make Ignatius of Antioch the villain who first introduced the cultic point of view with his extravagant metaphor about the eucharistic bread as "the medicine of immortality, the antidote that we should not die but live forever in Jesus Christ."[5] Ignatius was full of extravagant metaphors. His description of the Eucharist is only his stylistic way of stating the eschatological dimension of the Sacrament. In his letter to the Romans, he described his own martyrdom in Eucharistic terminology, quite after the manner of speaking in the New Testament: "I am God's grain, and am ground by the teeth of wild beasts, that I may be found pure bread."[6]

A better case could be made for apologists such as Justin Martyr and Tertullian, who saw the analogies between the Christian sacraments and the pagan mystery rites. Justin distinctly says that the bread and drink are not "common" once they have received thanksgiving by "the word of prayer that comes from Him," that is, from the Logos.[7] On the other hand, Justin's pupil Irenaeus used the same kind of language to refute the Gnostic heresy in its denial of the essential goodness of the created order of God; and he was horrified by the Gnostic treatment of sacraments as esoteric and magical instruments of grace.[8]

Another factor in the changing point of view was the typological application to the sacraments and the ministry of the Church of the whole cultic vocabulary of the Old Testament. Thus priestly and sacrificial terms came to be used of the clergy and of the rites over which they presided; and a

[5] *Ephesians* 20:2.
[6] *Romans* 4:1.
[7] *Apology*, I, 66.
[8] *Against Heresies* iv. 17. 5; iv. 18. 6; v. 2. 2–3.

distinction was made—unknown to the New Testament—between *kleros* and *laos,* clergy and laity, which has been with us ever since.[9] A recent study of Cyprian has attempted to show that this worthy Father of the Church was unfortunately advanced to the episcopate too soon after his conversion and without proper education in the Church's tradition of teaching. For it was Cyprian who exalted the potency of the Eucharistic species to work physical harm upon unworthy communicants, and who initiated the tendency to define the Church by reference to the hierarchy.[10]

The fourth and fifth centuries witnessed an intensification of the paradox, that as the Church became more and more involved in responsibility for the sanctification of the total life of society, it sharpened the distinction between the sacred and the profane. Many delayed their baptism even to the point of death, lest they defile the holy remission of guilt by post-baptismal sin. (It should be said, however, that responsible church leaders were not very happy about this custom.) In the case of the Eucharist, more and more emphasis was placed upon the awesomeness of the miracle of consecration. The invocation of the Spirit was now summoned upon the elements instead of upon the Church. One must approach them like

[9] The tendency seems to have started with I Clement (cf. chap. 40), but it is not established usage to refer *laos* to the nonordained "laity" until Clement of Alexandria (*Stromata* iii. 12. 90) and Tertullian (*Prescriptions against Heretics* 41). But when Tertullian passed over to Montanism, he rejected the distinction; cf. his famous tirade in *An Exhortation to Chastity* 7: "For are not we lay people also priests? . . . It is ecclesiastical authority which distinguishes clergy and laity, this and the dignity which sets a man apart by reason of membership in the hierarchy. . . . Obviously, where there are three gathered together, even though they are lay persons, there is a church."

[10] M. F. Wiles, "The Theological Legacy of St. Cyprian," *The Journal of Ecclesiastical History* XIV (1963), 139–49.

Moses before the burning bush, and gaze in dread before the
fire of divine Presence that makes the elements as it were
"live coals" upon the altar.[11] It is no wonder that the people
were more and more discouraged from communicating, despite
the exhortations of the clergy, and that the consecration of the
mysteries was finally withdrawn from sight behind curtains
and closed screens.

One could draw innumerable illustrations of the changing
perspective. A good one to consider is the development of
cultic places. We have noted that the primitive Church had no
sacred place of meeting—no word for a sacred building or
temple consecrated for cult purposes. Indeed the Church has
never lost entirely the sense of the appropriateness of using
any place, outdoors or indoors, above or below ground, for
the celebration of the liturgy, wherever it can assemble its
members. The "house-church" is still a reality among us. We
know from the apologists that one of the reasons for popular
charges of atheism against Christianity in the early centuries
was its lack of proper temples and cult edifices.[12] It is characteristic that Christian usage has applied the word *church* to
any gathering place where the Church comes together.

Even after the Church was able to erect special buildings for
its liturgical use during the long peace that extended between
the Valerian and the Diocletian persecutions, the old terminology was maintained. Lactantius, for example, consistently
speaks of the church buildings destroyed in the last great
persecution as *conventicula*, "meeting houses," for the true

[11] The tendency is very marked in Chrysostom, and his friend
and contemporary, Theodore of Mopsuestia. See the apt remarks of
Dom Gregory Dix, *The Shape of the Liturgy* (Dacre Press, 1944), pp.
480–85.

[12] Minucius Felix, *Octavius* 32; Clement of Alexandria, *Stromata*
vii. 5. 29.

temple of God (*dei templum*), said he, consisted of church people themselves.[13] After Constantine began the construction of magnificent edifices for the Church, the word adopted for them was *basilica,* "royal house," taken from the secular rather than from the cultic vocabulary of the age.

Ultimately, however, the Church developed a special form of the liturgy for consecrating church buildings, other than a dedication of them simply by the celebration of worship. The medieval orders of consecration of churches involve ceremonies of anointing and sprinkling with holy water as though the buildings were themselves being baptized and confirmed! Our own Prayer Book "Form of Consecration of a Church or Chapel," adopted in 1799, is to say the least an ambiguous compromise between a regular celebration of divine worship and a setting apart of the building "from all unhallowed, worldly, and common uses." But the prayer of consecration does recall the denunciation by the first martyr, St. Stephen, of the Jewish Temple, by reference to the prophetic word that the Most High "whom the heaven of heavens cannot contain" can "much less" be contained in "walls of temples made with hands" (cf. Acts 7:48–49).

It is, of course, a natural and appropriate instinct to show reverence to the places which by long association have been the focus of encounter with the living God and his Word and grace. But it can be carried to exaggerated extremes. Sitting as I do on the architectural commission of my diocese, I discover how difficult it is to persuade church building committees, who are planning the so-called "multiple purpose" structure— which will probably be torn down or entirely reconstructed before it is ever "consecrated"—that it is unnecessary to provide a screen or curtain to be drawn across the "sanctuary"

[13] *On the Death of the Persecutors* 15.

when they wish to use the nave for "unholy" purposes such as parish meetings or dinners. For why should the sight of the Holy Table and its furnishings be considered unfitting when the Church assembles to live its common life of work and mission? Certainly whatever is proper and fitting for Christian people to do together is proper and fitting for them to do in the presence of the "holy place."

There is a danger, one might say a blasphemous danger, in this cultic attitude toward the "holy place." There are, alas, some congregations that have so surrounded not only the building but the very liturgy that is celebrated within it with such taboos of what is thought to be seemly that they are unable to welcome in their midst baptized persons of other races or classes than themselves. And the converse of this is true also. There are parishes that would not dare to draw this distinction in the "holy place," but are prepared to draw it in the supposedly "unholy place" where other parish activities than those of worship take place. This, too, is blasphemy— to allow the outcast to eat of the Bread and drink of the Cup at the altar but not to invite him to partake of the Agape in a sandwich and a cup of coffee.

III] ONE of the consequences of turning the liturgy into a cult is that it becomes one among many objects that can be used for illustration and teaching of religion. Worship is made one among many, even though it may be the most important, resources for instruction in the faith. We inherit this approach to the liturgy from the Middle Ages. For example, the Western Church was unable to comprehend the theological significance of the iconoclastic controversy, and settled for the principle that liturgical art is not sacramental but decorative. Images and pictures are merely external vehicles for communicating a set of truths; they are the "Bible of the unlettered." The same notion was applied to the ceremonies of the liturgy; they were externalized as instructive instruments. Medieval treatises on the liturgy are full of this sort of thing—the allegorizing of the liturgy to teach doctrine and morals.

A typical example of this approach may be taken from the treatise on the liturgy entitled *Gemma animae* ("The Jewel of the Soul") by Honorius of Autun (d. *ca.* 1150):

The Mass imitates the conflict of a certain battle and triumph of victory. . . . Jesus our Emperor has fought with the devil and obtained for men the celestial republic that had been destroyed by enemies. . . . For the procession of the pontiff, clergy, and people is, as it were, the setting out of the Emperor and his army to war. They are attired with albs underneath and copes over them, or other solemn vestments, as soldiers about to fight who are protected with leather breastplates underneath and shields above them. When they go out from the choir they proceed as from a royal court. As the imperial banner and standard are borne in front by standard-bearers, so before us the Cross and banner are carried. There follow, like two armies, the singers advancing in order. Among them go instructors and precentors just as leaders of cohorts and inciters to war.[14]

So Honorius goes on with interminable illustration. Another of his interesting instructions is a comparison of the Mass to a judicial proceeding in a public court before judges. All of this was certainly a lively translation of the liturgy into the vernacular of the common life of the age. We should not throw stones. All of us have done the same kind of translation: for example, the way we use the Offertory of the Eucharist to illustrate the economic and political order of our times in and

[14] i. 72 (*P.L.* CLXXII, 566).

by which men make, distribute, buy, and sell bread and wine. Such instructions no doubt have their uses and values.

In a pamphlet published several years ago by our Church's national Department of Christian Education, entitled *Family Corporate Worship,* we were given this catechetical sample of question and answer:

Q. Why is Family Corporate Worship important to the Christian Education program?

A. This practice is necessary to the religious life of the home. It is a significant factor in the Christian education of children as well as their parents. In the repetition, week after week, of the services of the Book of Common Prayer throughout the Christian Year, worshipers are continually confronted with the major basic biblical doctrines and teachings of the Christian faith. Without the family pew, the church school courses . . . will be deprived of their liveliest access to the resources of the Church.

This piece is as true and as misleading as was the pedagogical reason Archbishop Cranmer gave in the Prayer Book for the appropiateness of public baptism—namely, that every man present would be thereby reminded of his own profession made to God in his own baptism. Obviously this is true. No one would deny it. But the purpose of the liturgy is not primarily one of instruction and edification—as this pamphlet comes dangerously close to implying.

Let it be said at once and unequivocably that the liturgy is an inexhaustible source of edification. I say *source,* not *resource.* For it is not one object of our reverent attention and use, however important and significant. The liturgy is the subject of God's own invisible action and working. In the liturgy God acts not only upon the Church but upon the whole world by his testimony to the accomplished work of Christ. This action is far deeper than our minds can consciously fathom or comprehend. In the liturgy the Kingdom is being brought into realization, and we are captured by it. The wall of separation is removed, sin is forgiven, the dead are raised up and made alive in the Spirit. Our response in contemplation of this "mystery" is indeed edification—that "mystery hidden for ages in God who created all things; that through the church the manifold wisdom of God might now be made known to the principalities and powers in the heavenly places. This was according to the eternal purpose which he has realized in Christ Jesus our Lord, in whom we have boldness and confidence of access through our faith in him" (Eph. 3:9–12).

If we set out, however, with the notion that the liturgy is a "significant factor" in an education program and the "liveliest access to the resources of the Church," we risk making it subject to a standard or norm outside of itself, whether this be the Bible, or the Faith considered as a set of doctrines, or perhaps some particularly idealized way of life. This was the disastrous trap into which the Reformation fell.

Having struggled valiantly to remove the old categories of "sacred" and "profane," the Reformers then proceeded to ecclesiasticize the liturgy again by making it subject to a norm of right doctrine unto edifying. But since they could not agree just what this right doctrine of the Scriptures was, they fell into dispute about the liturgy—whether it should be fixed or free, whether this ceremony was superstitious or "dumb" and that one not. I would not say that the Reformers, any less than their medieval forebears, would have denied that the liturgy exists to glorify God and testify to the redemption of the world. But their bitter and sorrowful controversies over stinted prayers and dumb ceremonies reveal how primary was the concern to make the liturgy teach an orthodox doctrine and a right ecclesiastical practice. We sometimes forget how much hortatory material was scattered through the Reformation liturgies—much of it now providentially removed or ignored. If we approach the liturgy as a chief means of edification, we risk a new kind of clericalizing of it, since only the experts decide what is edifying. At the same time, we cannot prevent the people from making their own individual and individualistic choices of what is edifying.

If attendance upon the liturgy makes a man into a good and sound and orthodox churchman, well and good. But that is a by-product. The purpose of the liturgy is to draw us into that redeeming action of God whereby in Christ he reconciles the world to himself. The liturgy cannot, any more than God, be shut up in a box, protected from the profanities of the world. The liturgy is not just a church activity, or a complex of esoteric religious teachings, even though only the Church celebrates it and only the man of faith understands it. It is open to the world, though the world acknowledge it not. It is celebrated for the world, though the world hold it in disrepute. The liturgy is God's mission to the world through his Church, until all is made up that is lacking in the sufferings of Christ, until all that is scattered abroad is gathered together into one (cf. Col. 1:24; John 11:52).

Yes, the Church has an altar, as the author of Hebrews reminds us—not an altar like that of the old tabernacle, with its rigid taboos of what is clean and what is unclean, what is acceptable and what is burned without the camp. For our altar was itself raised up outside the gate, outside the camp.

Therefore let us go forth to him outside the camp, bearing abuse for him. For here we have no lasting city, but we seek the city which is to come. Through him then let us continually offer up a sacrifice of praise to God, that is, the fruit of lips that acknowledge his name. Do not neglect to do good and to share what you have, for such sacrifices are pleasing to God. (HEB. 13:13–16)

5

The Knowledge of Christ
as Historical Person

1] "WHAT is time? Who can readily and briefly explain it?"—so queried St. Augustine in his *Confessions,* and added to his question:

We understand when we speak of it; we understand also when we hear it spoken of by another. What then is time? If no one asks me, I know: if I wish to explain it to one who asks, I know not.[1]

St. Augustine's query about time was, of course, unanswerable by definition in terms of its inner meaning; for its significance is part and parcel of the givenness of our creaturehood. The meaning of our creaturehood can only be finally answered by reference to him who created it but is himself uncreated, who created it in and with time, but who is himself without time. As our created being is but an image of his uncreated Being, so time as a condition of our creaturehood is but an image, in its fleeting present, of his everlasting presence.

We could make the same query and observation, in substance, if we ask, "What is the liturgy?" Just as it is fairly simple to define time externally to ourselves by reference to varied abstract systems of measurements, so it is easy to define the liturgy externally as a complex of orders, rites, and

[1] xi. 14.

ceremonies that regulate the common and corporate worship
of God. One could conceivably know all there is to know
about the liturgy in this external sense—its historical develop-
ments, its outward manifestations, its corpus of canonical and
rubrical law—and still one would not know the liturgy. It
would be comparable to a biographer who has all the vital
statistics, all the chronicle of sayings and doings, all the dating
and classification of sources oral and written, and yet does
not know his man—cannot, as we say, make him come alive;
and this, without regard to whether the biographer has actually
seen his subject in the flesh.

Questions of epistemology will doubtless be answered by
each individual according to his philosophy. For myself, I am
prepared to follow the instruction of St. Augustine, for his
statement of the problem seems to me convincing:

Nothing is learned even by its appropriate sign. If I am given a
sign and I do not know the thing of which it is the sign, it can
teach me nothing. . . . He alone teaches me anything who sets
before my eyes, or one of my other bodily senses, or my mind,
the things which I desire to know.

From words we can learn only words. Indeed we can learn only
their sound and noise. Even if words, in order to be words really,
must also be signs, I do not know that any sound I may hear is a
word until I know what it means. Knowledge of words is com-
pleted by knowledge of things, and by the hearing of words not
even words are learned.

We learn nothing new when we know the words already, and
when we do not know them we cannot say we have learned anything unless we also learn their meaning. And their meaning we
learn not from hearing their sound when they are uttered, but
from getting to know the things they signify. It is sound reasoning
and truly said that when words are spoken we either know or do
not know what they mean. If we know, we do not learn, but are

rather reminded of what we know. If we do not know, we are not even reminded, but are perhaps urged to inquire. . . .

We listen to Truth which presides over our minds within us, though of course we may be bidden to listen by someone using words. Our real Teacher is he who is so listened to, who is said to dwell in the inner man, namely Christ—that is, the unchangeable power and eternal wisdom of God. To this wisdom every rational soul gives heed, but to each is given only so much as he is able to receive, according to his own good or evil will.

If anyone is ever deceived it is not the fault of Truth, any more than it is the fault of the common light of day that the bodily eyes are often deceived. Confessedly we must pay heed to the light that it may let us discern visible things so far as we are able.[2]

I make no apology for so lengthy a quotation, for it sums up the way by which we know the reality of which we creatures participate. We know by signs, but these signs are intelligible and understandable only as we have experienced what they signify. And our judgments on these experiences, no less than our comprehension of them, depend upon our will to know, our love of truth, and our submission to the omniscient light of him by whom all things were made.

All education is discovery. It is discovery of a reality and truth that is already there before we are ever born, a reality and truth that will remain after we are gone. A teacher or an elder may serve as an incitement to this discovery by the pupil or the younger person, or may point him in the direction of discovery. But a teacher cannot make the pupil see, much less comprehend, what is there. A pupil always learns for himself and by himself. He learns by exposing his mind and directing his will toward that particular reality that he desires to know. He must commit himself; that is, he must have faith. Faith is

[2] *The Teacher,* 33, 36, 38.

always the ground of knowledge, of knowledge of reality as it is. "For whoever would draw near to God must believe that he exists and that he rewards those who seek him" (Heb. 11:6). Faith is not only the ground of our knowledge of God, or our knowledge of persons, but also of our knowledge of things, of the cosmos and the created world around and about us, of which we ourselves are indeed participants.

Looking at it from outside ourselves, we would say that reality reveals itself to him who would discover it. And because we are ourselves part of this reality, we are so made that we can communicate with it and know it. We may not know it exactly as we know our own existence. But insofar as we know it, we comprehend that it is related to the nature and character of our own existence. We can know the material world outside ourselves because we are ourselves part and parcel of the created order. We can know persons because we ourselves are persons. We can know God because we are made in his image, but more so because God has himself participated in our nature, having been made Man in the person of his Son.

This Augustinian view of education, which we have attempted to summarize—and to which we adhere—cuts through the division of educationists, and Christian educationists in particular, over the question of content-centered versus experience-centered (or, in current terminology, engagement-centered) methodology.[3] There is a delightful story about a famous Harvard divinity professor, in the days when "Religious Education" was struggling to find recognition as a legitimate discipline in the seminary curriculum. He is reported to have said, "Why should there be any problem about

---

[3] Cf. the first volume of the Bradner Lectures series: David R. Hunter, *Christian Education as Engagement* (Seabury Press, 1963).

religious education? All one needs to do is to decide what religion he wants to teach and then to teach it." One wishes that the problem was as simple as this! I have tried to teach Church history for over twenty-five years; and I think I have had reasonable success so far as getting my pupils through the "content-centered" canonical examinations. But how many of them have comprehended the significance of that content and its meaning for their own pastoral ministry I could not say.

The teacher's task is at best an endeavor to incite interest, to arouse engagement, to place the student in a light where he can see. But the student must see for himself. From some of my own teachers I have preserved nothing but a bibliography. From others I have notes that are constant well-springs of imaginative insight and interpretation.

II] OUR knowledge of history is one of the ways by which we extend and enlarge our knowledge of persons—what they did or did not do and say in the concrete situations of their own response to reality. This knowledge comes to us in two ways. There are records—what we call "sources"—writings, and monuments. These are never complete, and they are often inaccurate both in factual reporting and in their interpretations. Sometimes the surviving records are only partially intelligible to us. We may have difficulty in deciphering the language or the symbols and imagery in which these records are transmitted to us. Frequently, two or more persons engaged in response to the same situations record their facts and their interpretations differently, if not contradictorily. But the problem of knowledge of history lies not merely in the records themselves. Our knowledge is also conditioned by our own experience, not to say our own capacity to enter imaginatively into the situations of others. Even this capacity is relative to the patterns of thought, the questions asked or not asked, by the living, present community of persons who shape and mold consciously and unconsciously our lives.

History is all that we can remember—yet only what we can remember that relates itself significantly to our own present experience. Thus our knowledge of history is always relative and subject to constant revisions. Its reality is neither definitively complete nor perfect. Its sources are limited and partial. Our understanding of them is determined by our finite capacities and particular experiences, and by the concerns and interests of the society and generation whose life we share.

Our knowledge of the redeeming act of God in the concrete person of Jesus is in part comparable to the knowledge we have of any other historical person. We have records of what he said and did in the particular situations of his own generation, culture, and tradition. These records come from eyewitnesses or associates of eyewitnesses, and in this sense we classify them as primary sources. But the records are not mere chronicle. They are history—that is to say, interpreted chronicle—memories of a particular person transmitted through a community of persons with a particular faith. In the gospels we can never make a definitive separation of what is objective fact and what is subjective interpretation. We cannot separate Christ from his Church, any more than we can separate any man from the community of those who lived with him, responded to him, and loved him. The gospels are not merely records of Jesus; they are also records of the Church. And we are providentially fortunate that we have not one, but four such records, however baffling their contradictions of detailed reporting of facts and differences of imagery and style of interpretation.

Is it necessary to say again that the interpretations of meaning and significance vary not only among the several gospels, but within the traditions lying behind each several gospel, not to speak of the other New Testament documents? Is it necessary to insist that there can never be a definitive "Christology" that needs no revision of expression and interpretation? The New Testament writings convey to us a variety of responses to the person of Jesus, and of God as he is revealed in Jesus. All the devout and learned study and meditation on the records have not as yet produced a definitive and final exploration and unification of these responses into a single, consistent whole. Nor shall they ever do so, so long as time and history last, so long as there are persons still living and yet to be born who have not heard and responded to his person. Only in the last great Day, when we shall know even as we are known, and shall see him in the ultimate vision of his glory, shall we know his complete and perfect reality.

III] THE gospels present us with a number of images and terms by which we may endeavor to grasp and comprehend the meaning of Jesus' reality. Some of these require much labor of research for us to comprehend. Indeed it is difficult to know which of them, if any, Jesus himself would have accepted in his own consciousness of his own historical existence. For example, we are puzzled how to read with proper connotation the answer of Jesus at his trial to the high priest's question, or to Pilate's question, respectively: "Tell us if you are the Christ, the Son of God?" (Matt. 26:63) "Are you the King of the Jews?" (John 18:33) Does one read Jesus' reply, "You have said so," as an affirmative "Yes" or as a return of the question? Did he answer, "Yes, you have said what I am," or did he mean, "That is what *you* say"?

Let us assume, for the sake of argument, that Jesus believed himself to be the Messiah. It is at once apparent that he did not understand the concept and role of Messiah, as applied to himself, in the same way as did his contemporaries or even his disciples. We know that they understood the term as referring to a temporal king after the manner of David, the Lord's Anointed. But Jesus definitely rejected this understanding of his own destiny, even though he may have legitimately claimed blood descent from David. And what did the primitive Church make of the role and image of messiahship? At least we can say that as soon as the gospel was translated for the Gentile Greek, the term lost all relevance as the title of a role, and became a proper name. This change has virtually taken place even in the vocabulary of St. Paul, who certainly must have known what the word *Messiah* literally meant. Today the term *Messiah* has no meaning at all except to those who have some knowledge of its Old Testament background. And there are doubtless innumerable Christians today who love our Lord and worship and serve him devotedly (and who may listen every year at Christmas time to Handel's *The Messiah*), who do not know that "Christ" is but the Greek word for "Messiah." And if they did? How meaningful to their own experience is the figure of an anointed king in the Biblical sense of the term? We do have kings and queens in certain contemporary societies; and the English still anoint their sovereign at the coronation ceremonies. But although there is a definite relationship of concept, few would argue that Queen Elizabeth II bears in her person and role the fullness of meaning that Jesus and his contemporaries understood by "The Messiah."

We might make similar observations concerning other "Christologies" of the New Testament, such as that of "Son of Man" for example. Outside of the gospels, it occurs only once in New Testament documents (Acts 7:56), though it is undoubtedly related to the Pauline doctrine of Christ as the Second Adam (cf. 1 Cor. 15:45, 47), or to the vision of the Seer of Revelation of "one like a son of man" (1:13; 14:14). But when we meet the term in our hymns and prayers, those written and composed by contemporary Christians, its connotation is more humanitarian than eschatological—as in the hymn couplet:

> Above the noise of selfish strife,
> We hear thy voice, O Son of Man.

One need not deny, much less scorn, the truth and depth of meaning and insight in this modern use of "Son of Man"; but one has to admit that the associations of meaning are not exactly bounded by or coterminous with the Biblical understanding of these words.

It is tempting to say that the ecumenical Creeds provide us with a final and definitive statement of Christology. But these Creeds are final only in a limited sense. In the first place, they are affirmations, not explanations; and these affirmations are paradoxical. They mark out definite boundaries that exclude error; they do not resolve the mystery of the Person. Secondly, the Creeds, like the Scriptures, use symbolical language that can be understood only as one experiences the realities to which their images point. It was the error of Arius to take the analogy of the Father-Son relationship literally, because, as Athanasius pointed out, Arius could not imagine that God creates and begets after a different fashion than does man:

God is not as man, nor men as God. Men were created of matter and that passible; but God is immaterial and incorporeal. And if so be the same terms are used of God and man in divine Scripture, yet the clear-sighted, as Paul enjoins, will study it, and thereby discriminate, and dispose of what is written according to the nature of each subject, and avoid any confusion of sense, so as neither to conceive of the things of God in a human way, nor to ascribe the things of man to God. . . .

For God creates, and to create is also ascribed to men; and God has being, and men are said to be, having received from God this gift also. Yet does God create as men do? or is His being as man's being? Perish the thought; we understand the terms in one sense of God, and in another of men.

For God creates, in that He calls what is not into being, needing nothing thereunto; but men work some existing material, first praying, and so gaining the wit to make, from that God who has framed all things by His proper Word. And again, men, being incapable of self-existence, are enclosed in place, and consist in the Word of God; but God is self-existent, enclosing all things, and enclosed by none; within all according to His own goodness and power, yet without all in His proper nature.

As then men create not as God creates, as their being is not such as God's being, so men's generation is in one way, and the Son is from the Father in another. For the offspring of men are portions of their fathers, since the very nature of bodies is not uncompounded, but in a state of flux, and composed of parts; and men lose their substance in begetting, and again they gain substance from the accession of food. And on this account men in their time become fathers of many children; but God being without parts, is Father of the Son without partition or passion; for there is neither effluence of the Immaterial, nor influx from without, as among men; and being uncompounded in nature, He is Father of One Only Son. This is why He is Only-begotten, and alone in the Father's bosom, and alone is acknowledged by the Father to be from Him, saying, "This is my beloved Son, in whom I am well pleased."[4]

How much pain the Church would have been spared if churchmen of all generations, including our own, would understand that the Creeds are symbols! Recently a priest stood me down on the literalness of the Virgin Birth by shouting loudly that if a doctor had examined the Blessed Virgin after Jesus' birth he would have certified that she was a virgin. So what! What would a medical certificate have proved? (Thank God, we have no such certificate in the gospels!) It would prove only that a miracle had taken place, an extraordinary event. It would not prove the Incarnation. One has also to hold that he "was conceived by the Holy Ghost"; and no medical certificate can cope with *that* truth. Nor can the mind of man comprehend such a conception except by faith.

The Creeds also come to us conditioned by the language and patterns of thinking of a particular culture—specifically that of Greek thought, with its peculiar terms and connotations concerning essences and natures.[5] This culture is still our own today, though it has been very much attenuated, and we have increasing difficulties in comprehending its terminology. We simply cannot translate into modern vernaculars the word *hypostasis*. The modern concept of "person"—which ultimately derives from the psychological insight of St. Augustine[6]—does not really translate the notion of "person" held

---

[4] *Defense of the Nicene Definition,* 10–11.

[5] The best introduction is G. L. Prestige, *God in Patristic Thought* (S.P.C.K., 1952).

[6] See Paul Henry, S.J., *Saint Augustine on Personality* (The Saint Augustine Lecture 1959; Macmillan Co., 1960); also the great study of C. N. Cochrane, *Christianity and Classical Culture* (Oxford, 1940), pp. 399 ff.

by the Greek Fathers who formulated the Creeds in their original language.

Let us indeed be more bold. Christianity in history is no longer a purely Western religion. In the past hundred years it has penetrated ancient and rich cultures of the Orient, which have yet to make their contribution to the formulation of the Faith. It took two centuries for the confession of St. Peter, "You are the Christ, the Son of the living God," to be translated into the Greek theology of Origen concerning the eternal begetting of the Logos. It is not inconceivable that within another hundred years from the present, if God chooses to bring his Church into a new unity and synthesis of cultures and peoples, that our "coming great Church" might make a new creedal formulation, not in repudiation of the old ones— any more than the old Creeds repudiated the Scriptures—but in elucidation and enrichment of Western Christendom by the faith of the Church of the Orient.

6

The Reality of Christ
in the Liturgy

1] THE liturgy is for Christians another dimension of discovery in the knowledge of God as he is revealed in Jesus Christ. We have said that the Church worshiped before it had a Scripture or a Creed, that, in fact, both Scripture and Creed remain living instruments speaking to us in the here and now because they are borne in the context of the liturgy. The Church knows Jesus not only by the written record and interpretation of the New Testament. The Church knows Jesus in the remembrance of the living community that he brought into being by his word and deed.

Professor John Knox has argued this truth with convincing insight. He has pointed out, for example, that the Church remembers Jesus in significant ways that could not be proved merely by an external examination of the written gospels. Concretely, it remembers his moral perfection and his infinite love for his own. One may have indications of these all-important characteristics of his person from a reading of the gospels. But one can know them as *true* only from the inside, by participation in the communion of saints.[1] There is not

[1] John Knox, *The Church and the Reality of Christ* (Harper & Row, 1962), pp. 49 ff.

a one of us who cannot testify to the fact that the most convincing proof of the reality of Christ is his life in the lives of the saints whom we have known—and these, too, among all sorts and conditions of men.

This is why the philosophy of Christian education held in our Church today is very positive, and indeed very correct, in underscoring the fact that the quality of community life in our several parishes is paramount for the effectiveness of any formal instruction in church schools. A parish that does not live the gospel cannot witness to it. Of course, the grace of God can overrule even this. For God is not bound by any sin of man. If the Church does not witness to him, he will find his witness through the things that he has given to the Church, or he will, as he often does, witness to the Church from the world. Indeed we cannot rightly understand such renewal and reformation as the Church is undergoing in many quarters today except by acknowledgment that God is witnessing to it from the world. His prophets are not always communicants in good standing. Even when they are, their witness is often the more effective when it comes from a platform and a concern that we do not always or normally associate with the Church as an ecclesiastical institution.

The extension of justice in the racial tensions of our land has been initiated in the courts of law, not in the Church. This is a judgment upon the Church, surely, insofar as the Church has not, within the bounds of its own corporate life as an institution, displayed that oneness and unity of the races in Christ. But we must remember, too, that Christian laymen witness to their faith in the duties and vocation of the law. When Christian lawyers and judges act for racial justice in their professional duties, they are acting as churchmen in the world. The sad thing is that so many church people do not recognize this as a Christian witness but view it as a "secular" (that is, worldly) occupation, simply because the pronouncements have not come from specifically ecclesiastical assemblies.

But we know that God will judge his Church if it does not find means to witness within the social, economic, and political structures that affect the great masses of mankind in the technological and urban revolution of our times. The trumpet of the Church has as yet a very uncertain sound in the arena where most men are today struggling for order and justice and a richer life, as they grapple with problems of unemployment, automation, housing, public education, responsible representative government, and the like. These are not "secular" concerns. They are the very substance of Christ's ministry and service to the world.

The dimension of the knowledge of God in Christ that is revealed in the liturgy is not, however, merely the making present of the past revelation in the moral integrity of the believing community and its love for the brethren. This alone would not give the Church in its liturgy the right to its unique claims. The liturgy is not a rally to promote good causes. In fact, the welfare state can accomplish many of these at least more efficiently and more extensively, if not more lovingly, than the Church. Far from decrying the welfare state as demonic, the Church should welcome it, and faithfully witness within it that men are to be served and helped without ecclesiastical strings attached, if only because God made them and loves them even in their sin and alienation.

The extraordinary dimension of the liturgy is that of the future fulfillment—what we have called, in reference to the mission of Jesus, the realization of the Kingdom of God. The liturgy does not recall Jesus into the present as though he were a dead Socrates, whose beautiful example of selfless endeavor leading to martyrdom is cherished and promoted by loving and enthusiastic disciples, with the hope that they might share if not his earthly fate, at least his personal immortality. The liturgy is all this, to be sure; but if it is only this, it is dissolved in pietism and is consequently "good for nothing" in this world.

The liturgy is the realization of the Presence of the risen, ascended, and reigning Lord. As such, the meaning of the liturgy is hidden from the world and known only to the faithful. "He was known to them in the breaking of the bread" (Luke 24:35). The Church in the liturgy recalls and makes effective in the present not only the past redemptive act of Christ, but brings into the present also the glory that is to be revealed in the final consummation. In the liturgy the Church is lifted up into the heavenly sphere where Christ lives and reigns. It passes out of time and history into eternity. In the liturgy the Church discovers the Kingdom of God, and becomes most truly what it is called to be by the purpose of God, transformed and transfigured.

At the Last Supper, Jesus inaugurated the Kingdom by the earnest of the giving of himself in entire oblation to God and in selfless service to his disciples, that by this perfect offering of love unto the uttermost, his sacrifice should avail "for many," that is, for the reconciliation of the world. In the prayer of Gethsemane and the obedience of the Cross he sealed this giving unto reconciliation forever, and in the Resurrection manifestation at the first Easter Eucharist the accomplishment of this reconciliation was revealed to and discovered by the Church in the presence of him who is indeed the firstborn among many brethren. In the Eucharist the Church knows by immediate experience and involvement the nature and character of the life of the world to come, for it comprehends at last the perfect freedom of him, with all who belong to him, who reigns because he serves.

The gospel is its own best commentary on the meaning of the liturgy. By his teaching and ministry, Jesus transformed the expectation of Israel and of his disciples that the Kingdom would be manifested by a hierarchy of rank. He revealed it as a distinction of service. Israel would not be a kingdom to which all other nations and peoples would pay honor and tribute, but a Suffering Servant. The disciples would not sit at his right hand and his left in seats of privilege, but would achieve greatness only by the entire oblation, unto a baptism with him in death if need be, in lowly service. Thus the scandal of Jesus to the world, to Israel, and to his own disciples, is the scandal that makes the liturgy incomprehensible, if not offensive, to the world—and, alas, even to many who are formally at least within the Church.

Jesus lost his popularity when he refused the earthly crown, and would not let the crowd take him by force and make him king (cf. John 6:15, 66–69). He lost his life because his love broke the bounds of religious respectability when he ate and drank with "publicans and sinners." His teaching perverted the official and orthodox conception of the Kingdom, by his insistence that the outcast and the unclean would not only be invited but would respond without reservations to the Messianic banquet. He almost lost his disciples because he would not take up the sword, and he let himself be betrayed into the hands of the Gentiles. Thus his mind was not "conformed to this world but . . . transformed . . . [to] prove what is the will of God, what is good and acceptable and perfect" (Rom. 12:2). Was there ever a better and more insightful comment and application of this transformation in place of conformation than that of St. Paul to the Philippians?

Do nothing from selfishness or conceit, but in humility count others better than yourselves. Let each of you look not only to his own interests, but also to the interests of others. Have this mind among yourselves, which you have in Christ Jesus, who, though he was in the form of God, did not count equality with God a thing to be grasped, but emptied himself, taking the form of a servant, being born in the likeness of men. And being found in human form he humbled himself and became obedient unto death, even death on a cross. Therefore God has highly exalted him. . . .
(PHIL. 2:3–9)

"Do nothing from selfishness or conceit, but in humility." So we are told by the Third Evangelist (22:23–24) that at the Last Supper, immediately after Jesus gave himself in the bread and the cup, he warned them of betrayal,

And they began to question one another, which of them it was that would do this.

That is, there was not one of them with him there at that Table who understood the meaning of what was happening— any one of them might have been the traitor—because, as the evangelist goes on to say,

A dispute also arose among them, which of them was to be regarded as the greatest.

This is indeed a very unlovely picture, but one we dare not forget. There, at the very inauguration of fulfillment, one witnesses the final conflict, with the sin embedded even in the most loyal and faithful of disciples—a strife as to who should be the greatest in the promised Kingdom.

The discourse of Jesus that followed this dispute (Luke

22:25–30) occurs in the other Synoptic gospels in slightly different contexts (Matt. 20:25–28; Mark 10:42–45), but nonetheless in the context of the dispute that rent the disciples as they followed Jesus all the way up to Jerusalem—the dispute that was openly confessed when James and John made their request for the chief seats.

"The kings of the Gentiles exercise lordship over them; and those in authority over them are called benefactors. But not so with you. . . ."

Indeed one marvels today, even in their ruins, at the great public monuments and benefactions of the Caesars and the Herods, and all the other great ones who received acclamation, even worship, for their worldly gifts—the bread and circuses, the baths and libraries, the courts and temples. Who would deny the faithful disciples the hope and expectation of such a role in the coming Kingdom of God? But Jesus did.

"Let the greatest among you become as the youngest, and the leader as one who serves. For which is the greater, one who sits at table, or one who serves? Is it not the one who sits at table? But I am among you as one who serves."

The Fourth Evangelist expresses the same teaching in the scandal of the foot-washing. That Jesus should have stooped to perform this menial service of a slave was indeed a scandal to his disciples, and the more so since not one of them had thought to do it for him, much less for one another. So when Peter objected in the name of them all, Jesus answered:

"What I am doing you do not know now, but afterward you will understand." Peter said to him, "You shall never wash my feet." Jesus answered him, "If I do not wash you, you have no part in me." Simon Peter said to him, "Lord, not my feet only but also my hands and my head!"   (JOHN 13:7–9)

That was the Baptism of the apostles—the total washing and submergence in the water that Jesus serves.

But to return to the discourse at the Supper as recorded by the Third Evangelist—we find Jesus continuing with most extraordinary words:

"You are those who have continued with me in my trials [*or,* temptations].

At least, up to that moment they had continued, though they were soon to forsake him and flee. And what are these trials, these temptations? They are the very ones that pursued him from his baptism by John to the agony of Gethsemane—the temptation to accept conformation to the world's understanding and expectation of the Kingdom, the temptation to be ministered unto rather than to minister. Ministry, service, *diakonia*—this word sums up everything. The terrible trials and temptations of the Evil One are only conquered and overthrown by the "service" that is the true manifestation of the presence of the Kingdom.

So Jesus now explicitly made his one and only institution:

"As my Father appointed a kingdom for me, so do I appoint for you that you may eat and drink at my table in my kingdom, and sit on thrones judging the twelve tribes of Israel."

Thus the upper room became the scene of an enthronement—so different from the audience halls of the Caesars! There, as it were by an anticipation, the availing intercession was first made by the one true Priest, who at the same time was the one obedient Servant—the intercession for Peter, that though Satan sift him like wheat, his faith should not fail; the intercession for all who should believe and keep his word, that they might be one, and that they might behold the glory that the Father had given to the Son (cf. Luke 22:31–32; John 17:9 ff.).

It is in this institution of the Kingdom that we most fully grasp the fact of the Real Presence in the Eucharist. It is the disclosure by Christ and the discovery by us of the ultimate reality, which is the consummation of all things that God has prepared from before the foundation of the world (cf. Eph. 1:3–14). One does not need to argue any doctrine of the Real Presence. One has only to unveil the covering of mind and heart and will to behold that he is there, ready to serve us before ever we can serve him, remembering us before ever we remember him, interceding for us before ever we can intercede through him for the reconciliation of many.

The rabbis had taught that the Kingdom would come when Israel obeyed the Law. In Jesus' perfect love the Law was fulfilled, and in him the representative Son, Israel called to be God's Son and to glorify God in its obedience, has finally become obedient and fulfilled its calling and destiny. From henceforth the good news is no longer awaited, but is proclaimed as having come. We are literally in "the last times," because our citizenship is now in heaven. The gathering in of the Gentiles is as surely the sign of this eschatological age as is the outpouring of the Spirit by which it is accomplished. The liturgy is the mission in and through which the old alienation is overcome, and we savor, if it be only for fleeting moments, only as long as the celebration lasts, the communion of saints.

We have affirmed that Jesus did not come to reform an old religion or found a new one. He did not establish a new cultus to replace the old. He simply transformed it by fulfillment. For this reason, I am inclined to side with those scholars who deny that the Last Supper was a Passover, and affirm that it was an ordinary meal of friends. Of course, it had points of contact with the Passover experience. It was a domestic, family celebration. It was a celebration of a great deliverance. But it was a form of family celebration where the father of the household is prepared without shame, without self-concern, without losing any dignity, to serve the need of even the youngest and most helpless member. There is no longer any special time or season when this fulfillment of loving service cannot be celebrated. The Eucharist, unlike the Passover, is not tied to special times and seasons. It can be properly accomplished at any hour of day or night, on any day of every year, wherever two or three are gathered in his Name. The Daily Office and the Christian Year extend its thanksgiving for the new creation and redemption to the sanctification of the totality of time and the vocation of everything that is in heaven, or on earth, or under the earth.

In concluding this exposition, I would like to posit a question, for which I am not prepared to give an answer that would satisfy a theologian. It is a question that I am often asked by both clergy and laity, a question that I find as exciting as it is disturbing. It is this: "What is the difference, if any, in the Real Presence of Christ in the Eucharist and his presence in any other worshipful act where two or three are gathered in his Name and agree in his Name, or his Presence in the works of mercy and compassion that are done in his Name and for his sake?"

Obviously there is a difference of external form. But the revelation and discovery is the same, for surely it is the same Christ, giving himself to meet the need of whoever comes to him in faith and love and true repentance. But the real point of the question, I believe, is its reminder that the liturgy cannot be separated from the mission, the worship cannot be distinguished from the merciful service. At the Resurrection, both the women's and the disciples' immediate reaction to the sight of him was, as the evangelists remind us, one of worship, reverence, and awe. But what the Lord said was simply, "Go and tell."

A Church that is not on mission is not a Church, however orthodox its doctrine, however sumptuous its cult, however respectable its behavior. For the veil is still before its eyes, and it thinks that Christ is safely locked and hidden in the tabernacle. But when Jesus cried, "It is finished," the veil of the Temple was rent in twain from the top to the bottom, and the very graves of the dead were opened.

Thus the acceptance and completion of his obedience was the revelation of his glory—of him

> the faithful witness,
> the first-born of the dead,
> and the ruler of kings on earth.

To him who loves us and has freed us from our sins by his blood and made us a kingdom, priests to his God and Father, to him be glory and dominion for ever and ever. Amen.
Behold, he is coming with the clouds, and every eye will see him, every one who pierced him; and all tribes of the earth will wail on account of him. Even so. Amen.   (REV. 1:5–7)

* * *

After this I looked,
and behold, a great multitude which no man could number,
    from every nation,
    from all tribes and peoples and tongues,
standing before the throne and before the Lamb,
    clothed in white robes,
    with palm branches in their hands . . .

These are they who have come out of the great tribulation;
they have washed their robes and made them white in the
    blood of the Lamb.

Therefore are they before the throne of God,
    and serve him day and night within his temple;
    and he who sits upon the throne will shelter them with his
        presence.
They shall hunger no more, neither thirst any more;
    the sun shall not strike them, nor any scorching heat.
For the Lamb in the midst of the throne will be their shepherd,
    and he will guide them to springs of living water;
    and God will wipe away every tear from their eyes.

(REV. 7:9, 14–17)

PART

II

Reconstruction
of the
Liturgy

7

Conditions
of Reconstruction

1] IN PART ONE we have attempted to approximate a definition of the liturgy. It is a comprehensive, all-encompassing instrument, composed of creaturely signs of word and action, which God uses for the re-creation of the world through the reconciliation of all things in Christ. The liturgy is the means whereby God enables us, who live in the created order of time and space, consciously and intently to overcome the rebellious, fallen, and corrupt condition of this creation, and to lay hold with a "sure and certain hope" upon the perfection and consummation of the world to come. In the liturgy we experience redemption: namely, the forgiveness of sin, that is, a victory by which all that has been at enmity is now at peace; and the restoration of a good will, that is, a holy communion by which all that has been alienated is made capable of service.

Thus the liturgy is the realization of the fulfilling of the law—both the law of joyous obedience in the original condition of our creaturehood before the Fall, and the law of painful obedience exacted in the laborious conditions of our history after the Fall. The liturgy is the realization of life in the Spirit; and "the fruit of the Spirit is love, joy, peace, patience, kindness, goodness, faithfulness, gentleness, self-control; against such there is no law" (Gal. 5:22–23).

Words fail us in every attempt to describe adequately and fully this discovery and experience of ultimate reality. One suspects that this is the reason why the tradition has left us no indubitable eyewitness accounts of the Resurrection of Christ. For who can describe the end of the world—the "end" not only in the sense of the end of time, but also in the sense of the end of purpose? We cannot be certain that any of the gospels as we have them was written by an eyewitness. Even St. Paul, an incontestable albeit by his own admission the last and least of the eyewitnesses (I Cor. 15:8–9), confines himself to a bare catalogue of the Resurrection manifestations. If, as some scholars believe, he was referring to his own experience of the Resurrection in II Corinthians 12:1–5, he says only that he cannot tell whether it was an experience "in the body" or "out of the body," when "caught up into Paradise" there were "heard things that cannot be told, which man may not utter."

The Fourth Evangelist, who may or may not have been an eyewitness, has perhaps given us the simplest and most intelligible account of the manifestation when the disciples were gathered together on the first Easter Day:

Jesus came and stood among them and said to them, "Peace be with you." When he had said this, he showed them his hands and his side. Then the disciples were glad when they saw the Lord. Jesus said to them again, "Peace be with you. As the Father has sent me, even so I send you." And when he had said this, he breathed on them, and said to them, "Receive the Holy Spirit."

(20:19–22.)

This is a description of the Resurrection. But is it not also the simplest and most perfect account of what happens in the

Eucharist?—communion and peace between God and man and between man and man, that passes understanding; commission to bear the Lord's own service of love to the uttermost reaches of the world; and enablement to comprehend this peace and to bear this service by the indwelling of the Holy Spirit.

The best we can do, therefore, is to denote the liturgy, at least from our creaturely point of view and the limitations of our human words of communication, as joy and peace, praise and thanksgiving. For by such words as these we signify the experience of reconciliation. By such words as these we acknowledge our participation by grace in "the powers of the age to come" (Heb. 6:5). So the Seer of Patmos saw by revelation on the Lord's Day—whether Sunday or Easter or the final Day of the Lord, we cannot say which—the vision of the City of God coming down from heaven as a ceaseless paean of joyous praise in endless Alleluia.

We have also attempted to suggest, by reference to the insights of St. Augustine, that Christian education finds its purposeful end in the discovery of this ultimate reality as it is illuminated and actualized by God in Christ in the liturgy. The liturgy is not one among many resources of Christian education. The liturgical experience of reconciliation and service is both the origin and the goal of our Christian education and edification. All the techniques of education, whether by spoken or by printed words and signs, whether in group discussion or in individual study, are fundamentally only analysis and application of the liturgy. The liturgy is not a cult, if by cult we mean a complex of sacral objects and actions whose holiness must be kept separate in strict taboo from all profane objects and actions. Such a conception of liturgy is nothing less than a Gnostic and Manichaean dualistic heresy, which is perhaps the most persistent as it is the most dangerous enemy of the gospel.

Through the liturgy all creation enters into sanctification—all material things and all interpersonal relationships of identification, communication, and service. The liturgy makes holy all the ordinary actions of washing and anointing, of signing and sealing, of eating and drinking, of laying on of hands and exchanging the kiss. For the Apostle has warned us about "disputes over opinions":

One believes he may eat anything, while the weak man eats only vegetables. Let not him who eats despise him who abstains, and let not him who abstains pass judgment on him who eats; for God has welcomed him. . . .

One man esteems one day as better than another, while another man esteems all days alike. Let every one be fully convinced in his own mind. He who observes the day, observes it in honor of the Lord. He also who eats, eats in honor of the Lord, since he gives thanks to God; while he who abstains, abstains in honor of the Lord and gives thanks to God.   (ROM. 14:2–3, 5–6)

II] AT THIS POINT it seems best to make a digression upon the question of corporateness versus individuality in the liturgy. It is fashionable today in all discussions of liturgy to emphasize its corporate character and to stress the importance of active participation by all the people worshiping. This emphasis is proper and good, and very much needed, even in the so-called liturgical Churches which have forms of worship that presuppose this participation.

But the coming together of people and their formation into an interdependent community must be understood as always initiated and accomplished by God. Only by his Word and Act are they made into a "royal priesthood" and "God's own people" (I Peter 2:9). Yet one often receives the impression that the people themselves create this community by what they do with and for one another, if not with and for God, so that the liturgy is turned into a kind of celebration of "togetherness" that may pervert it into a respectable covering for the conformity of a social club. However desirable it may be for the individual worshipers to be socially acquainted and on the friendliest terms, it is not necessary for them to be so in order to participate. For no matter how much the individual is tied to his fellow worshipers by affectionate bonds of friendship and concern—and such ties do greatly enhance the joy and edification of worship—ultimately each individual must face and bear confrontation with the presence of God in the intimacy and mystery of his own personal concreteness.

The address of God in the liturgy is made to each one of us in the crisis of our own individual aloneness, alienation, and agony of decision, when we are aware of and attentive to the fact that we are being addressed by God. It is one of the great services of the liturgy to protect the individual from the humiliation of this exposure and the destructive consequences of being naked to the gaze and curiosity of those who, however friendly disposed, may surround him in this encounter. This is why all forms of corporate worship that violate the privacy of the individual in this crisis cannot be sustained, and certainly should not be deliberately promoted—such as open penitential disciplines, speaking in tongues, and many revivalistic techniques. If they are promoted and fostered, they inevitably issue in sectarian schisms that rend asunder the community.

On the other hand, the liturgy, in preserving the individual from humiliation, at the same time enfolds, sustains, and heals him by relieving him from the despair of his isolation, since it does encompass him in the loving communion of a great "cloud of witnesses"—witnesses he may or may not know face to face. He is knit into the intercession and supplication of a supernatural community of all times and places, in the Holy Catholic Church that transcends and transfigures all his natural relationships and communities. It is "in Christ" that the walls of partition are broken down. It is only "in Christ" that we can comprehend how there is neither male nor female, bond nor free, Jew nor Greek, white nor black.

Our Church today makes much effort to encourage its members to restore the family pew, to attend worship together as families, even to the point of communicating communicant members of a family simultaneously with a blessing on non-communicant members of the same natural family. There can be no fundamental objection to this, since God intends to redeem the family as a family no less than its individual members as individuals. We are taught and we believe that the family is a sign of the Church, and that the love of husband and wife signifies to us the love that is "betwixt Christ and his Church." We understand, too, that this overt and constant focus upon the family is a necessary part of the Church's pastoral ministry in a society such as ours that provides the Devil with so many subtle ways of warfare against its stability and fidelity.

But we must also remember that in the Resurrection "they neither marry nor are given in marriage, but are like angels in heaven" (Mark 12:25). We must remember, too, that many members of the Church as yet belong to families divided in their ultimate allegiances. It is membership in "the household of faith" that sanctifies membership in earthly households, whether of one or of many members, and not vice versa. This should be obvious, yet it is apparently not obvious enough to rid us of the sentimental nonsense of denoting certain liturgical gatherings as "family services," as though other liturgical assemblies were not, or of promoting "corporate communions" for men as distinct from "corporate communions" for women or even such absurd designations as "the Children's Mass."

One could make similar observations respecting the natural distinctions of race that present our generation of Christendom with such crucial concern. We must hope and pray and work for the extension of justice in our common society of differing races, if only for prudential and humanitarian reasons. But in the Church such natural and creaturely reasons must be transformed and transcended by obedience to the new commandment that we love one another even as Christ has loved us. The integration of the races in the one Body of Christ, nourished and nurtured by one and the same supernatural food and supernatural drink, should manifest and actualize a reality that is more than courtesy and forbearance and justice.

The liturgy summons us to a community that is rooted not in a reasonable morality but in a reckless and uncalculated service. The failures of the Church today to witness to its faith that God has indeed in Christ made us all "of one blood" are due to its feeble sense of mission. The problem is to persuade our congregations not only to permit or to allow the outcasts to share with us the crumbs of the Lord's Table, but to seek them out, to invite them—indeed, shall we say, to "compel people to come in" (Luke 14:23).

III] IN OUR STRESS upon the priority and initiative of God in the liturgy, we do not overlook the fact that he risks giving to his Church what the Thirty-nine Articles calls "power to decree Rites and Ceremonies." In the Old Testament, the law of liturgical observance in rites and ceremonies was considered even in minute details a revelation that made the earthly tabernacle and temple but an image of a heavenly model. Hence the ceremonial law was as unchangeable and inalterable as the moral law. Of course, it did change in the transient history of the people of God, as they passed from their wilderness wandering to settlement in Canaan and entered into the exchanges of cultic influence and counterinfluence with their neighbors. The cultus was subjected to revisions, reformations, and enrichments. But the theory of its fixation by divine decree was never abandoned. In principle the outlook of Moses and of Ezekiel was not essentially different.

Some of the prophets, notably Jeremiah, had intimations of the transitory nature of the cult, and indeed of its corruptibility. But it is remarkable, no less, that the cultus of the Old Covenant, thanks to the doctrine of inspiration, remained through the centuries so basically the same. This is true despite the wealth of detail and casuistry about its observance developed by the priests and rabbis that we know from the traditions of the *Mishnah,* and the allegorizing and spiritualizing interpretations of it that we read in an apologist such as Philo. But the rite performed by Jesus with his disciples in the upper room would have been more readily identifiable by Israelites who had participated in the Passover for a millennium than the High Mass of a medieval cathedral would have been recognized by the apostles as identical with the Last Supper—at least in its outward form of expression.

It is one of the strongest arguments for the view we have maintained—namely, that our Lord fulfilled all cultic observance when he brought in the Kingdom—that the Church has continually in history changed and reformed the outward and visible expressions of its worship, and has accepted their relativity "according to the various exigency of times and occasions." The Preface of the Prayer Book specifically acknowledges this fact as "a most invaluable part of that blessed 'liberty wherewith Christ hath made us free.' "

It is true, the Church has not always changed its liturgical forms consciously or even willingly. But major reformations and enrichments of its worship have generally been made deliberately, and justified by appeal to the continuing inspiration of the Holy Spirit. There have been times, also, when reformers of worship, in an overly zealous endeavor to conform to some law of worship according to the Scriptures, attempted to restore a pattern of cultus identical with what was supposed to be the worship of the New Testament Church. But they have never succeeded in winning over to their view the majority of Christian believers. Liturgical movements that are merely archaeological are unconvincing, if not irritating.

We shall not be suggesting any radical revision of our inherited theological notions about what is called the essential form and matter of the sacramental liturgies. It is conceivable, though most unlikely, that the Church might substitute some other element than water in the administration of Baptism. The Church has, however, varied in its use of running water or still water, and more significantly in the amount of water employed in the ministration. In fact, the amount of water remains an occasion of contention among Christians. The Church is not likely to abandon the use of water, even if it should abandon an interpretation of the New Testament that posits a specific institution of it by the Lord, simply because the tradition from the very beginning has universally acknowledged it as the proper element. It is proper because the signification of water most perfectly expresses the meaning of Baptism as both a washing and a drowning.

Nor is the Church likely to alter the form of Baptism in the

Name of the Trinity, although we have some evidence that in the earliest days many baptisms were administered in the Name of Jesus only. The old liturgies also show differences in the precise way the Name of the Trinity was applied. It was somewhat different in rites that demanded a triple immersion from those that assumed a single immersion.

Likewise with the Eucharist. The use of bread and wine will continue to be maintained by the majority of Christians, apart from any belief in a formal institution, simply because that is what our Lord himself used at the Last Supper. Some ancient schismatics substituted water for wine; some modern schismatics substitute grape juice. There was a startled look on the face of certain representatives of the Protestant Churches at a meeting of a subcommittee of the Consultation on Church Union when the representatives of the Episcopal Church would not recognize the validity of a Eucharist that did not use wine. On the other hand, I must confess that I had considerable sympathy for the plea of a Japanese churchman, whom I met several years ago, who asked whether it was not legitimate in the circumstances of his own country's culture and economy to substitute rice-cake for wheat-bread and saki for grape-wine.

The essential form of the Eucharist is a more thorny problem. Our Episcopal Church was until recently on record (Canon 36[1]) in maintaining that a prayer of thanksgiving which includes the Words of Institution and an Invocation of the Holy Spirit is essential. Compared with the theological position of other ancient Christian communions, this is a good example of Anglican ambiguity. I suspect that any acceptable liturgy in a reunited Church will contain all that Anglicans

[1] This was altered, however, at the General Convention in 1961, when Canons 36 and 38 were revised and combined.

ask. But, again, there is no one, final, fixed way of formulating the prayer of thanksgiving. The wording of the Institution narrative differs in all the Catholic liturgies, and it seldom conforms to the differing accounts of the New Testament word for word. The Invocation of the Holy Spirit has also undergone numerous modifications both in language and in meaning. It does not even occur in the Roman liturgy, if it ever did—but I for one am not prepared to say that the Roman Mass is not a valid Eucharist. Of greater concern, I think, is the loss from the ancient tradition of the invoking of the Spirit upon the Church, no less than upon the elements. For the primary purpose of the *epiclesis* is that the Church in the Eucharistic action might know itself to be fulfilled with the Holy Spirit and therefore participant in the Age to Come.

There is emerging another way of looking at the form of the Eucharist, and that is to embrace within the term the total action, which involves not only the Consecration but the preparation in the Offertory and the consummation in Communion. The Eucharist is, after all, a meal, even though it has been attenuated ceremonially into a token meal. Very few would desire to return to the primitive association of the Eucharist with a regular full meal, for it is absurd to suppose that the visible and tangible measurement of the amount of food and drink could make any difference to the invisible and infinite grace that is conveyed. But theologians have their quibbles. A Roman Catholic friend was telling me that in discussion of the *schema* on the liturgy prepared for the Second Vatican Council there was altercation as to whether the draft should speak of the Paschal *convivium* or the Paschal *sacrificium*. The two words have in the course of centuries of theological elucidations taken on differing connotations. Yet if we have learned anything about the primary meaning of *sacrifi-*

cium, it is that it was originally a *convivium.* In the case of the Passover specifically, it is hard to see how one could separate, even though one might distinguish, the *sacrificium* from the *convivium.*

8

Proposals For Reform

IN PRESENTING certain observations for the reconstruction
of the liturgy, we are frank to say that our proposals are not
definitive. They are arguable; but they are not concerned
with quibbles over petty matters of detail. They are rooted in
principles that already inhere in the liturgical inheritance of
the Church. It is relatively easy for a liturgiologist to propound
ideal solutions, without regard to very intractable cultural and
sociological conditions within which clergy and people live
and operate. We only approximate ideal conditions. It is better
therefore for the liturgiologist to seek out the right questions,
before he gives his answers. No revision of the liturgy is worth
the effort if we do not try first of all to be as certain as we can
about the principles that underlie our inheritance; and then
we can ask where the evolvement of the liturgy should proceed,
whether by subtraction or addition or by transformation.

Major shifts or innovations in the structures and forms of
expression of the liturgy cannot, of course, be safely pre-
dicted. That such things may come is both possible and probable. In another context I have mentioned the fact that we
await significant contributions from the younger Churches of
the non-Western world to enrich our theology and our spirituality. They will doubtless in God's good time do the same
for the liturgy.

1] WE MAY BEGIN by reference to the Christian Year. The pattern of the Christian Year has remained basically unchanged for 1300 years—ever since the definitive settlement of the Latin liturgy in the time of Pope Gregory the Great. It represents a creative synthesis of two cycles: one based on the lunar calendar of the Jews that is pivoted in Easter (the Pascha); the other based on the solar calendar of the Graeco-Roman Gentiles that is pivoted in the old winter solstices of Christmas and Epiphany. The primary cycle is, of course, that related to Easter; and this has a connection with a spring New Year. This at once shows that the natural foundation of the Christian Year comes from a culture of the northern hemisphere.[1]

For the past half-millennium Christianity has also been planted in the southern hemisphere, where the natural seasons are in reverse relative to the northern hemisphere. This in itself might be a reason for considering proposals for a fixed date of Easter: to detach it from the inevitable associations of springtime criteria of calculation. Be that as it may, we have yet to see what impact upon the calendar will come from the cultures of the Far East, which have not been tied to the calendrical systems of the Graeco-Roman world.

We do not suppose that Easter is likely to be shifted to a date other than that of our spring. But it may be that we shall see the end of associating Easter with the springtime renewal of nature, which provides so much of the vivid imagery of Christian praise and devotion, and its detachment as a purely historical commemoration. Christmas has certainly lost most

[1] It is true that certain ancient calendars had an autumn New Year; but in the period of the emergence of Christianity, both Jews and Gentiles of the Roman Empire began their religious calendars in the spring.

of its old associations with the winter solstice. Easter need not suffer by disassociation from the spring moon.

One of the most common bits of instruction prevalent in the Church is the teaching that the first half of the Christian Year, from Advent to Whitsunday, recalls our Lord's life; and the other half, the Trinity Season, recalls his teaching. Thus the Christian Year is often justified as a form of catechesis. This is sheer nonsense. The Christian Year is a mystery through which every moment and all the times and seasons of this life are transcended and fulfilled in that reality which is beyond time. Each single holy day, each single gospel pericope in the sequence of the year, is of itself a sacrament of the whole gospel. Each single feast renews the fullness and fulfillment of the Feast of feasts, our death and resurrection with Christ. It is the more difficult to make this clear so long as we perpetuate, through an accidental event in the history of the medieval Church in England, the naming of the Sundays following Pentecost as Sundays after the special and singular Feast of the Trinity. This peculiarity is the reason why many think that one half of the year recalls history, the other half recalls doctrine or teaching.

The Christian Year does have two halves, and these are the complementary halves of Advent to Pentecost and Pentecost to Advent. Each year thus fulfills the whole history of years. Pentecost divides the history of the world, of this created world, as seen from the perspective of the history of salvation (*Heilsgeschichte*). It also divides the first and second Advents of the Lord, but ties them together in inseparable bonds.

Let us remember that the ancient Church named the whole fifty days from Easter to Whitsunday as "Pentecost," for it embraced the climactic revelation of Resurrection, Ascension, and outpouring of the Spirit. The first half of the Christian

Year moves forward to this climax; the second half, in full assurance of this first Advent, moves forward to its perfect consummation in the final Advent. Thus each Christian Year interlocks with the next one following. In actual, chronological time, we are living today—in this year of grace 1965—between the first Pentecost and the last Advent. But in the mystery of existence in the Christian transcendence and transfiguration of time, we live in the totality of all that is encompassed between first Advent and Epiphany and final Advent and Epiphany.

This mystery we understand by reason of the gift of Pentecost—the mystery so beautifully expressed in the Collect of Trinity IV: that "we may so pass through things temporal, that we lose not the things eternal." Alas, Cranmer mangled this Collect by an unwarranted insertion that makes it read, that "we may so pass through things temporal, that we *finally* lose not the things eternal." The Christian Year, however, makes present to us here and now all that is final and ultimate. The liturgy is not a discipline that prepares us step by step for some future goal and reward. The liturgy is at any time and in any place that goal present and real *now*. If indeed, as we have attempted to show, the Kingdom comes in the liturgy, then God's will is done in the liturgy on earth as it is in heaven. This realization of joyful obedience is final, though it needs to be renewed in us every day of this temporal and mortal existence.

There are a few lesser matters in the Christian Year that need re-examination. One of them concerns the Pre-Lenten Season, which was instituted in the sixth century at Rome as privileged Sundays of solemn supplication in response to a particular historical crisis. But their propers maintain many relics of an Italian season of seedtime, with their gospel par-

ables of the Laborers in the Vineyard and of the Sower. This
latter theme is taken up again in the concerns of the Rogation
Days before Ascension. For the Rogation Days were instituted
in Gaul, a more northerly region where seedtime came later
than in Italy.

This is an unnecessary duplication. It would be better to
remove the liturgical observance of this natural season of sow-
ing and seeding from the sequence of the Proper of Time,
whether before Lent or before Ascension, and make it a mov-
able and adjustable Votive comparable to its counterpart in
the Harvest Festival that our American liturgy associates with
Thanksgiving Day. Thus Rogation Days and harvest Thanksgiving Days could be made adaptable to their respective seasons in the natural order of man's work in any part of the
world. They would not then be tied to the rhythm of this
natural order of seasons in the northern hemisphere, much
less in the Mediterranean world.

At the same time, we would eliminate the necessary interruption of the great fifty days of Eastertide—or, if you prefer,
of Pentecost—by the insertion of three "days of solemn supplication," which the Prayer Book lists for the Rogation Days
under the Table of Fasts. There should be no fasting in Eastertide. It is a curious anomaly that we have eliminated the fast
between Christmas and Epiphany, but keep it on Easter Fri-
day, indeed throughout the Fridays of Eastertide.

The removal of the Pre-Lenten Season would make it possible to link more definitely the post-Epiphany season and the
pre-Easter season that we call Lent. We should then be able
to see the significance of the ancient sequence of Sunday gospels that runs from Epiphany to Holy Week. These were
originally the great Johannine signs of death and resurrection,
beginning with the Baptism of Jesus and his First Miracle at

Cana and ending on Passion Sunday with the Raising of Lazarus. The only interruption might possibly be the gospel of the
Transfiguration on the Sunday before Lent, and the Temptation story on the First Sunday of Lent.

Our Lenten Sunday gospels preserve very little of this important and significant sequence leading up to Easter. Actually
we preserve only the pericope of the Feeding of the Multitude
on the Fourth Sunday of Lent. But we should restore such
outstanding Johannine gospels as the Samaritan Woman, the
Discourse with Nicodemus, the Healing of the Crippled Man
at the Pool of Bethesda, the Healing of the Man Born Blind,
and the Raising of Lazarus. Such gospels as these would provide the best way of pilgrimage from Epiphany to the Passion
and Resurrection. They would hold together the inevitable
relation of our Lord's baptism in water and in Spirit (Epiphany) and his baptism unto death in blood and Spirit (Holy
Week). They would make each Sunday in this sequence a
proclamation of death and resurrection, and incidentally restore the Johannine signs of this mystery to their proper liturgical sequence and context.[2]

Lastly, but by no means least in importance, the restoration

[2] The Standing Liturgical Commission has made a preliminary
proposal looking toward the restoration of this Johannine sequence in
Prayer Book Studies XII (Church Pension Fund, 1958), pp. 95–109.
To date it has received no comment from the Church about the matter!

I have been greatly helped to see the significance of the ancient
Johannine sequence of gospels by two studies: R. J. Hesbert, "Les
dimanches de carême dans les manuscrits romano-bénéventains,"
Ephemerides liturgicae XLVIII (1934), 198–222, and C. Callewaert,
"La Quaresima a Milano al tempo di S. Ambrogio," *Ambrosius* VIII
(1932), 273–82 (reprinted in *Sacris Erudiri*, 1950, 549–60). From a
quite different (that is, nonliturgical) approach, I have been greatly
stimulated by the discussion of C. H. Dodd, *The Interpretation of the
Fourth Gospel* (Cambridge, 1953), pp. 297 ff.

of the sequence of Johannine signs would revitalize Lent as a season—not merely of penitence and discipline, but as a season of renewal by an intensification of emphasis upon the Way of the Cross. We would thus have a restoration of the wholeness of the gospel that points, in each stage of the way from Incarnation to Pascha, to the revelation that in his great humility in taking upon himself our flesh and suffering death upon the Cross, the Lord manifested forth his glory, a glory that includes his taking captivity captive and making it partaker of his Resurrection.

II] THE mystery of the Christian Year that incorporates all of time into the once-for-all and eternal fulfillment of the Paschal–Pentecost event is itself a frame for the liturgy of Christian Initiation. In the ancient Church the initiation of the sacramental mysteries of Baptism and Confirmation and first Eucharist were normally administered only at Easter and Pentecost. Exceptions were necessarily made at whatever moment of time a catechumen found himself *in extremis,* that is, in the very existential experience of death and resurrection. Later, the administration of the initiatory rites was provided at any time or season, because of the extension of infant baptism and the (existential) risk of infant mortality. When this happened, the initiatory rites were broken into three stages— into a kind of process of initiation that extended over a period of time the several experiences of Baptism, Confirmation, and admission to the Eucharist. This shattering of the unity of the Paschal mystery has had the unfortunate result of undergirding, though perhaps not actually causing, the division of Christendom. The sad fact is that no two major branches of the several Christian traditions agree either in their theology or in their policy of Christian Initiation.

As is often the case, the Eastern Churches remain more faithful to the original custom of administering the entire initiation at once, normally to infants. The Roman Catholics, through a series of what one might call historical accidents, have set a pattern of threefold rite for all of Western Christendom. But the several traditions of Western Christianity are, to say the least, in a muddle about the process, and exhibit almost every variety of sequence and of emphasis, except for a common agreement as to the priority and necessity of Baptism. Some baptize infants, others do not; some admit to communion before Confirmation, others do not; some require episcopal Confirmation, others do not. And in our own Anglican tradition there is perhaps the greatest muddle of all, the divisions of teaching about the meaning and significance of Confirmation, both as it relates to the grace of Baptism and as it relates to the privilege of communicant status. This diversity is intolerable. But there is hope that in the extensive ecumenical debate and discussion regarding Christian Initiation that has been going on for the past two decades, we may arrive at larger agreements.[3]

No one can claim, at the present stage of dialogue, any definitive solution. What I have to offer is done with considerable hesitation, for it is extremely difficult to keep together all the facets of the problem and arrange them with convincing logic. It would be more simple if ideal solutions based purely on theological considerations could be adopted. And theological considerations are basic. But dogmatic theology divorced from pastoral theology is sterile. The complications of

[3] An enormous literature on the subject has been produced in recent years; but it may suffice to point to the remarkable report (with an excellent bibliography) of the Faith and Order Commission on Christ and the Church, edited by Keith Bridston, *One Lord, One Baptism* (Augsburg Publishing House, 1960).

our contemporary problem stem largely from pastoral concerns. The Church today is a mixed lot of committed, half-committed, and only formally committed persons and families. In theory the great dividing line between the redeemed and the unredeemed is Baptism. But in actuality, certainly in the Anglican tradition, the more obvious line of demarcation is in the commitment of Confirmation. We are more and more distressed by decisions as to what infants of what parents to baptize, and the age when such baptized infants should be confirmed and admitted to the Eucharist. We fool ourselves if we think that Anglicans do not in practice, if not in theory, magnify Confirmation at the expense of Baptism.

An illuminating illustration of our situation lies in a story told by Archbishop Leslie Brown of Uganda at the Liturgical Consultation following the Anglican Congress in Toronto. He described a certain occasion in an English parish when the bishop arrived to administer Confirmation. The rector informed the bishop that he should go to his place in the sanctuary and wait until he, the rector, administered Baptism to certain of the candidates and then bring them all forward to be confirmed. The bishop's reply was that the rector would do nothing of the kind. For it would simply exhibit a conception of Baptism as a mere preliminary to the more impressive —and episcopal—rite of Confirmation. On the contrary, said the bishop, "I shall myself preside over the baptisms at the font, as well as administer Confirmation."

This story has helped my own thinking about principles involved in our problem. Let me say, first of all, that as an Episcopalian I am not prepared to dispense with bishops. I believe episcopacy to be one of God's great gifts to his Church, and that it is essentially a sacrament of the Church's temporal and visible unity. The bishop is, if nothing else, the minister of Orders in the Church. But the Orders of the Church, as Dr. F. S. Cellier has incisively reminded us, are *four,* not three.[4] The laity is also a Holy Order. They are not profane, as some self-important clerics seem to imply by their love of status and privilege. The laity is the fundamental Holy Order in the Church, and all of us are made laymen in our Baptism. We must rid ourselves of all the common parlance that suggests that Confirmation is the so-called "ordination of the laity." Baptism is the layman's ordination. Confirmation strengthens what is given in Baptism, our personal relationship to God the Holy Spirit and the Church in which he indwells, that we may be responsible witnesses to the faith that is in us.

The first step, therefore, in the reconstruction of the initiation liturgy, would seem to me one that restores to the bishop his presidency and office in the *total* initiation of the Christian, and not just in that part we call Confirmation. Indeed, I should go so far as to say that there is more meaning in the episcopal office, succeeding from that of the apostles, when it is viewed as a mission to preach and baptize than when it is restricted to a duty to visit and confirm. There is no good reason why we should not reintegrate in one single rite Baptism, Confirmation, and admission to the Eucharist—whether this is done for infants or for adults, depending upon the pastoral needs in these respective cases.[5]

A Christian should be fully initiated once for all, for at whatever age he undergoes this experience, whether in infancy, childhood, adolescence, or adulthood, he will need Christian

[4] F. S. Cellier, "The Liturgical Movement and the Ministry of the Laity," *The Eucharist and Liturgical Renewal,* edited by Massey H. Shepherd, Jr. (Oxford, 1960), pp. 87–114.

[5] This seems to be the direction of thinking of the Liturgical Commission of the Church of England, judging from its report *Baptism and Confirmation* (S.P.C.K., 1959).

nurture for the rest of his life. It is spiritually healthy for a child to grow up in the household of faith with the full privileges of the family, and eat and drink at the family table. We learn the significance of the Eucharist by experience of its communal integrity before we are capable of understanding its implications by any analytical instruction. The early Church was right in withholding the catechetical lectures on the sacraments until after the candidates had been initiated. We can inform and instruct people in the meaning of the Eucharist as long as we wish, but they will never comprehend it until they are knit together in the experience of it. Practically considered—and we can learn something here from our Roman Catholic and Orthodox brothers—we would not lose any more, and would probably lose less of our confirmands from continuing, responsible witness, if we incorporated them at a much earlier stage, if not in infancy, into the fullness of life of the Church.

The lovely custom of the bishop as chief pastor visiting all his flock to participate with them in the liturgy could be made the appropriate time for Baptism, Confirmation, and Eucharist all in one. Whatever the day or hour, whether Sunday or a holy day or some other day, this fullness of the liturgy of the people of God with their chief apostolic pastor would point to and manifest the Easter–Pentecost reality. Of course, this happens in every single Baptism, in every Confirmation, and in every Eucharist. But there are advantages of witness, and certainly of edification, in exhibiting the wholeness of the Mystery.

One reason why we hesitate to make this reintegration is the holdover of the Augustinian notion—which none of us any longer believes—that unbaptized infants who die have no hope of salvation. As much as I love and admire St. Augustine,

I regret his baleful influence in this hideous doctrine that makes God less loving than ourselves. It is not necessary for us to hasten little infants to the font lest by some mishap they go to limbo. But if any should still be possessed by this demonic doctrine, there is a very simple solution available. We could restore the form of Admission to the Catechumenate,[6] by enrolling the name and signing with the Cross. Thus the catechumen, should he die before his Baptism, would undoubtedly be saved by the Baptism of desire.

III]   I SHALL not say much about the problem of reconstruction of the Eucharistic liturgy.[7] We would all agree with a remark made to me by a member of the Church in Wales, who said that our American Prayer Book form is "certainly a celebrant's rite." We have all been exposed to celebrations where it would seem not to be very important whether there were any people present besides the priest or not—performances to stimulate the devotion and piety of any who might be present, but not requiring of them any responsible participation by making an offering or even by communicating.

Part of the problem lies in the unimaginative use of what our own liturgy already makes available; part of it in needed revisions of its structure and language so that it moves more dramatically and logically in the sequence of parts and in the involvement of the congregation. For example, there is no good reason for the celebrant to read the lessons if other readers are available. There is no good reason for excluding the people from all the offertory actions.

[6] Such forms may be found in the South African and Indian Prayer Books.

[7] I may refer to my remarks on this matter in my Bohlen Lectures, *The Reform of Liturgical Worship* (Oxford, 1961), pp. 91 ff.

Two observations may be made. The first is that the Eucharist is a feast, a banquet, a festal occasion. It should always be celebrated with the fullest splendor and joy of which the assembly is capable. I cannot see any justification for a spoken celebration with a congregation that is capable of song. I cannot see any justification for a celebration in which the priest monopolizes the whole rite when there are other Orders of Ministry present, such as laymen, deacons, and bishops. There is also much to be said in favor of the revival of "concelebration" in cases where more than one priest (or bishop) are present at the celebration.[8]

Part of our problem lies in the confusion in our church about what liturgies are catechetical, what are ascetical, and, for want of a better term, what are sacramental. The Ante-Communion is catechetical; the Daily Office is ascetical; and the Eucharist proper, from the Offertory to the end, is sacramental. But we are constantly mixing these purposes, probably because our congregations are so mixed with the committed, half-committed, and the uncommitted. Yet we shall destroy the magnificence of the Daily Office if we continue to use it for evangelism instead of using the Ante-Communion.[9] And we abuse the Eucharist when we employ it primarily for ascetical devotion.

All of this results from an approach to worship and liturgy primarily as a means of edification. The clergy then become entrepreneurs of what are called "worship services," while

[8] A very good discussion of concelebration may be found in Basil Minchin, *Every Man in His Ministry* (Darton, Longman and Todd, 1960), Part Two.

[9] This use of the Office for evangelism is responsible for the many proposals (and practices) of revising it, by substituting hymns for the canticles, omitting one lesson, and generally oversimplifying the lectionary and use of the Psalter.

the laity pick and choose what they think are spiritual bargains. Many Episcopal parishes on Sunday morning look today like nothing so much as liturgical shopping centers attached to a school. The so-called "family service" that serves as a preliminary or follow-up to the classroom is the greatest variety store of all. We shall not unscramble this messiness until we begin to put the right people into the appropriate liturgy.

Beginners, including the uncommitted, need something like Ante-Communion, with its simple proclamation of the gospel and exposition of it. Ante-Communion is the evangelistic liturgy. (Of course, I assume that it shall have an adequate lectionary and employ a modern translation of the Bible.) Those who are already committed but need consistent nurture and strengthening—and that includes most of us—should find the answer to their need in the sacraments; for the sacraments were given to sinners, not to saints. And then the more advanced, those more ready for what the Alexandrian Fathers would have called "true Christian gnosis," can find the Daily Offices an inexhaustible treasure of spirituality, and a properly balanced one, for it is the Church's prayers and praises.

Secondly, and this sums up all we have tried to say, the liturgy is tested by its fruit—not that God is tested, but that he tests us. The liturgy does not exist to soothe the spiritual aches and pains and give peace of mind. It does not exist even to bring order and beauty into life and elevate taste. It does all these things. But the liturgy exists primarily to inform a Christian's vocation in the world, and to set him on fire for mission.

It is good to have the recent warning of a Roman Catholic layman to all who love the liturgy and work for its renewal that, though "we do not teach the social dimension of worship in order to bring about a commitment to social justice, . . . if increased social awareness and compassion do not follow from liturgical renewal, there is reason to question the realism of the movement."[10] We Episcopalians in particular need to be reminded that though we may have an incomparable liturgy, or, if not incomparable, at least comparable in its Scriptural and Catholic spirituality to that of any other liturgical tradition in Christendom, we make a very poor showing as a Church in evangelistic, missionary, and charitable zeal when compared with Christian bodies less privileged in their worship than we have been for four hundred years.

Mission is implicit in the liturgy, but our liturgical forms do not always make it explicit. The principal weakness of the form of celebrating the Eucharist contained in our Prayer Book is that this explicit summons to mission is lacking. We pray for those in need and any other adversity, but within a context that subsumes this intercession within a prayer for the Church rather than for the world. We confess our sins against the "Divine Majesty" but not so positively against our fellow men. We supplicate God for "grace and heavenly benediction" and for the divine indwelling, but not so clearly for obedience to the divine commission. And at the end we receive a blessing and not a dismissal. Thus, far too many churchmen find the liturgy a refuge from the world rather than a breakthrough to the world.

On page 72 of the Prayer Book—following the proclamation of the good news in Law and Epistle and Gospel and Creed and Sermon—we begin our response in the Eucharistic mystery when the Offertory Sentence is announced. It is good

---

[10] R. G. Hoyt, "Liturgy and the Social Order," *The Revival of the Liturgy,* edited by F. R. McManus (Herder and Herder, 1963), pp. 147–48.

to ponder upon the first word there set forth—that stray saying of our Lord that survives as it were by accident in the Book of Acts (20:35), a saying that is no less a marvelous summary of the whole meaning of the gospel and of the liturgy:

> Remember the words of the Lord Jesus, how he said,
> It is more blessed to give than to receive.